AEROSMITH

(Ian T. Tilton/S.I.N.)

AEROSMITH

THE FALL AND THE RISE OF ROCK'S GREATEST BAND

MARTIN HUXLEY

ST. MARTIN'S PRESS
NEW YORK

AEROSMITH. Copyright © 1995 by Scott Schinder. All rights
reserved. Printed in the United States of America. No part of
this book may be used or reproduced in any manner whatso-
ever without written permission except in the case of brief
quotations embodied in critical articles or reviews. For information, address St. Martin's Press, 175 Fifth Avenue, New
York, N.Y. 10010.

Design by Junie Lee

Library of Congress Cataloging-in-Publication Data

Huxley, Martin.
    Aerosmith : the fall and rise of rock's greatest band /
Martin Huxley.
        p.   cm.
    ISBN 0-312-11737-X
    1. Aerosmith (Musical group)   2. Rock musicians—
United States—Biography.   I. Title.
ML421.A32H8   1995
782.42165'92'2—dc20
    [B]   94-43923
                                                        CIP
                                                        MN

First Edition: March 1995

10 9 8 7 6 5 4 3 2 1

ACKNOWLEDGMENTS

The author would like to thank the following individuals, without whose advice, encouragement and/or support this project would have been an even bigger ordeal than it was: Jill Christiansen, Drew and Meryl Wheeler, Madeleine Morel, Jim Fitzgerald, Evie Greenbaum, Dave Dunton and Regina Dunton, Holly George-Warren, Ira Robbins, Maria Castello, Liane Hentscher, Jim Bessman, Keith Moerer, Kathy Gillis, Matt Sweeney, Jeremy Tepper, Cindy Toth, Michelle Freedman, Eric Ambel, Bruce Bennett, The Hound, Phast Phreddie Patterson, Bill Flanagan, Ted Mico, Jason Cohen, and Michael Krugman.

CONTENTS

1

EAT THE RICH

On August 16, 1991, Columbia Records—the flagship label of Sony Music, the world's largest music-entertainment conglomerate—put the brakes on several months' worth of heated music-industry speculation by announcing the re-signing of Aerosmith. The deal, which would return the band to the label that was the scene of its groundbreaking commercial triumphs during the 1970s, immediately set entertainment-biz tongues fluttering. And with good reason.

Even in a business built on extravagance and overkill, one in which superstar record deals have scaled increasingly outlandish heights of financial excess, the new Aerosmith-Sony arrangement was a remarkable one. Although no financial specifics were officially disclosed, the six-album deal is worth a reported $30 million—imposing figures even by inflated nineties standards. Even more impressive was the fact that the contract wouldn't even take effect for several more years, since the band still owed at least two more studio albums to Geffen Records, the company that had helped engineer the band's multiplatinum late-eighties comeback.

In other words, Sony was paying megabucks, up front, for the privilege of releasing new Aerosmith product beginning in 1998 or so. By that time, Steven Tyler, the band's oldest member, would be fifty years old, and Brad Whitford, the youngest, would be forty-six.

Not bad for a band whose career had, just a few years earlier, been written off by most of the music industry as a hopelessly drug-devastated disaster area. In the space of two decades, Steven Tyler, Joe Perry, Brad Whitford, Tom Hamilton, and Joey Kramer had, against all conventional logic, succumbed to and survived virtually every imaginable rock-star pitfall, squandered untold millions on drugs, alcohol, and all manner of personal and professional indulgences, and somehow emerged from the ordeal miraculously intact.

The first decade of Aerosmith's recording career had seen the group spectacularly claw its way to the top of the rock world and fall from grace in equally epic fashion, collapsing in a bitter, drug-clouded haze that eventually left frontman Tyler and guitarist Perry, the band's visual and musical core, creatively bankrupt and financially strapped. Yet, with the original Aerosmith lineup's re-formation in the mid-eighties, the group miraculously pulled itself together to reemerge not only clean and sober, but bigger and—in the eyes and ears of many—better than ever.

"Our story was basically that we had it all, and we pissed it all away," Joe Perry said, looking back at the band's exploits from a nineties perspective. An all-too-common story in the temptation-filled rock world. The difference in Aerosmith's case is that they lost everything and somehow won it back.

"We believed that anything worth doing was worth over-doing," Steven Tyler has said, and indeed, Aerosmith's personal and professional excesses effectively torpedoed the band's career. Now, they were reaping the bounty of a comeback that was equally over-the-top.

Under the circumstances, the line "You've got to lose to know how to win," from the band's immortal anthem "Dream On," had a distinctly resonant ring. . . .

2

MOVIN' OUT

"In my mind I was always a rock star," Steven Tyler has said more than once, and that observation helps put his success into perspective. Indeed, if there's one consistent theme in Tyler's career, it's that relentless self-belief that's always driven him, even when his other vices left him at rock bottom.

It was only natural that music would be the vehicle for Steven's natural drive. Born Steven Tallarico in New York City on March 26, 1948 (though he's sometimes given his year of birth as 1952), he grew up in a middle-class family headed by his father, Victor Tallarico, a Juilliard-trained classical pianist who'd performed at Carnegie Hall and who earned his living teaching music in New York City's public school system. A generation earlier, Victor's grandfather Giovanni was a cellist who'd performed in chamber ensembles in some of Manhattan's ritziest hotel ballrooms during the 1920s.

"I grew up under the piano," Tyler recalled in a 1990 interview with *Musician* magazine. "My father talked to me with his fingers, playing Debussy and Beethoven. He didn't talk to me much one-to-one as a human being, but I'm glad he didn't. That's where my emotion comes from."

Emotion was something that young Steven possessed plenty of. During a less-than-stellar academic career at Roosevelt High School in Yonkers, New York, the budding drummer and singer—who was frequently beaten up by bigger kids who called him "Nigger Lips" in honor of his already prominent mouth—displayed the same curious combination of intelligence, imagination, and lack of discipline that's sent many an educational career down the rock 'n' roll road.

With a distinct aversion to authority and a pronounced penchant for mischief, Steven was well on his way to low-level juvenile delinquency, joining a local gang called the Green Mountain Boys. ("We were the Robin Hoods of Yonkers," he later recalled.) By his early teens, he'd discovered marijuana and a variety of other forbidden substances—still novel pursuits for a suburban high-school student during the first half of the sixties.

It was just that sort of extracurricular activity that eventually got Steven thrown out of Roosevelt High. "They put a narcotics agent in our ceramics class, see," he told *Rock* magazine. "*He* had the best weed around. He used to turn us on during lunchtime." Steven and his friends didn't learn that their new classmate was an undercover Putnam County deputy sheriff until a squad car showed up in the Tallarico family's driveway and the cops handcuffed the budding pothead right in front of his parents.

The bust landed Steven in court, where—with the sort of persuasive panache that would serve him well later in life—he sweet-talked the judge into reducing the charges and letting him off with a misdemeanor. The whole sordid affair got Steven expelled from Roosevelt High, and he ended his formal education at Quintano's, a private school for creative but unruly kids.

In a 1975 interview with *Circus* magazine, Tyler described Quintano's as "a school for young artists, the kind of school you pay an awful lot of money to go but where you don't have to show up. I went to school three days out of five and wound up most of the time in the park with the chickie-doos. So I passed that with flying colors. That was the extent of my schooling."

As a teen, Steven spent his summers in the rural environs of Sunapee, New Hampshire, where his parents owned and operated Trow-Rico Lodge, a 360-acre summer resort. It was in Sunapee that he began channeling his creative impulses into performing in comic skits during Saturday-night talent shows at Trow-Rico and, more significantly, as drummer in his dad's Lester Lanin–style swing band, with whom Steven played at a more upstate local hotel, the Sunapee Lodge.

But any thoughts the young Tallarico may have had about a career as a swing-band drummer went straight out the window when the British Invasion hit American shores. Inspired by the Beatles and the wave of U.K. guitar bands that had followed them onto the U.S. pop charts, he formed his first "serious" group, the Strangeurs, sometime in 1964. With sixteen-year-old Steven doubling on drums and lead vocals, the Strangeurs began life as a typical mid-sixties cover combo, specializing in renditions of material by such contemporary Brit combos as the Beatles, the Rolling Stones, the Animals, and the Yardbirds. When a similarly-named Manhattan band surfaced, Tallarico's combo briefly amended their moniker to Thee Strangeurs, before settling on the snappier handle Chain Reaction. Along with the new name came an influx of original material, written by Steven in collaboration with the band's keyboardist, Don Solomon.

Chain Reaction diligently worked the small-time club circuit through New York and New England, plying their stylishly derivative, anglophilic pop-rock and reportedly playing their self-appointed rock-star roles to the hilt. But the stylishly attired quintet's attempts at translating its modest club-level success into a recording career proved frustrating. A pair of quietly released singles—"The Sun"/"When I Needed You" (for the Date label), and "You Should Have Been Here Yesterday"/"Ever-Loving Man" (on Verve)—went nowhere.

The Tallarico composition "When I Needed You," recorded October 5, 1966, at CBS Studios in New York, later resurfaced on Aerosmith's 1991 retrospective boxed set *Pandora's Box*. The track, a fairly straightforward pop offering with some mild trendy psychedelic touches, gives some insight into Chain Reaction's accessible but overly imitative style. On listening to the song nearly a quarter century after its creation, Tyler recalled "how excited I was about being in an actual recording band. It was a total dream come true. The other side of it is that it's a pretty lame song. I never got a cent."

Early in his musical endeavors, the teenaged Tallarico discovered a second home in the fertile musical community of New York's Greenwich Village. It wasn't long before the middle-class misfit was spending most of his free time in the Village, where he enthusiastically embraced the chemical, sexual, and musical freedoms that the burgeoning scene had to offer.

"We'd leave Westchester four o'clock Friday afternoon and take the subway down and spend all night there," Tyler recalled in a *Circus* interview. "We'd buy a bottle of Rock Rye, sit in the park and get faced, and walk the street like everybody else. I used to stuff my face at the Tin Angel, went to the Night Owl, saw the Spoonful there, the Fugs. I played at the Bitter End, the Bizarre and the Cafe Wha? . . ."

In the course of his adventures in the Village, Tallarico fell in with the members of the "baroque-pop" group the Left Banke, who'd scored a massive hit with their 1967 debut single "Walk Away Renee," but were now foundering for direction without their original songwriting mastermind Michael Brown. While the Left Banke's chart clout had waned considerably since their initial triumph, their influence on the ambitious Tallarico—who ended up singing backup on "Desiree" and "Dark is the Bark," both on the band's 1968 album *The Left Banke Too*—was immediate and indelible.

"They had a hit under their belt, a million-seller nationwide, and they were just the laziest mothers ever . . . . I played a couple of gigs with them, and watched them flush themselves down the toilet," he later recalled. "I'll never forget being in their apartment one day and one of them saying, 'What's the date today? Are we recording tonight? What are we going to record?' It turned out they were. 'Don't worry, we'll come up with something.' I couldn't believe they were taking it so lightly. I remember thinking, 'There's got to be a better way of doing this.' "

Though his experience with the Left Banke further strengthened Tallarico's career resolve, success continued to elude Chain Reaction even as their original repertoire and stage act grew more professional and streamlined.

The group even got to play occasional high-profile gigs opening for the likes of the Byrds, the Beach Boys, and—perhaps most significantly—the last-gasp 1968 lineup of the Yardbirds, in which guitarist Jimmy Page was road-testing the rudiments of the heavy-metal style he'd soon perfect with Led Zeppelin. Chain Reaction opened four shows for the 1968-model Yardbirds, including a March 30 concert at New York's Anderson Theater, which was recorded and eventually released as the legendary *Live Yardbirds* album (which was deleted soon after its 1971 release when Page threatened litigation).

But these scattered scraps of encouragement weren't enough to sustain Chain Reaction's dwindling momentum, and the band eventually fell apart. Tallarico and writing partner Solomon formed a new, short-lived outfit, William Proud, which similarly failed to improve their fortunes. In the summer of 1969, frustrated with his inability to crack the New York big time, Tallarico hitchhiked to his parents' place in Sunapee, little suspecting what fate had in store for him. . . .

3

ONE WAY STREET

Like his future bandmate Tallarico, Joe Perry—born Anthony Joseph Perry on September 10, 1950, in Lawrence, Massachusetts—hailed from a musically inclined middle-class family. But, for all of his parents' attempts to interest him in classical training, Joe had his sights firmly set on earthier musical pursuits. He'd been attracted to rock 'n' roll since his early childhood, but, as with so many others of his generation, it was the arrival of the Beatles that awakened him to the possibilities of playing electric guitar. After an unenthusiastic stab at high school and a similarly unsuccessful stint in prep school, Perry gave up on mainstream education. He spent the next two years working a frustrating minimum-wage factory job, before deciding to try his luck in New Hampshire, where his parents, too, had a summer home.

"I can remember when I was younger, a certain feeling would happen when I would turn music on and it would take me away, make me feel good," Perry recalled in a 1980 *Creem* interview. "I can remember when I was working in this factory after dropping out of prep school. I'd wake up in the morning and I wouldn't drink any coffee or take any speed, I'd just put on Ten Years After's 'Goin' Home,' and I'd be up and moving for the rest of the day. Ever since, I've always wanted to do what they did, and have it in my head and be able to control it."

In New Hampshire, Perry worked a variety of part-time jobs, including one washing dishes in an ice-cream parlor where Tallarico and his fellow Chain Reaction members were frequent customers (and rather obnoxious, unruly ones at that). He also met and befriended a blond-haired local bassist named Tom Hamilton, who possessed the distinction of having been arrested in Sunapee's first-ever acid bust.

Thomas William Hamilton was born on the last day of 1951 in Colorado Springs, Colorado. His father's career as a civilian Air Force employee meant that the Hamilton family moved frequently during Tom's childhood. By the time the family settled in New Hampshire, Tom was a rabid Beatlemaniac, eventually joining the Mosquitos, a high-school combo whose entomological handle made clear their admiration for the Fab Four.

By 1966, Hamilton and Perry formed a combo with the self-effacing handle Pipe Dream, which by the end of the decade had evolved into the harder-edged, blues-based Jam Band, a rough and raunchy outfit specializing in covers of tunes by the likes of the Yardbirds, Cream, Ten Years After, and the MC5. Though something less than a professional package, the Jam

Band embodied an anarchic blend of energy, speed, volume, and sheer unbridled craziness.

It was exactly those qualities that impressed Steven Tallarico after Perry invited him to one of the Jam Band's gigs at a Sunapee club called The Barn, where Chain Reaction had often played and where the Jam Band was virtually the house group. To the enthusiastic but relatively unworldly Perry and Hamilton, the more experienced Tallarico, with his cocksure attitude, fashionable Carnaby Street threads and streetwise career drive, was a Pro, or as close to one as they were likely to come.

"Steven sure looked like a rock star, and he *definitely* acted like one," Perry recalls, "so we just assumed he already was one."

"I mean, Steven had already put out a *record,* for God's sake," adds Hamilton. "He was the real thing. That was the ultimate to us."

"Steven knew how to keep things tight," Perry affirms. "We didn't have a clue about discipline. For us the whole thing was all about feel. So we needed each other."

If Perry and Hamilton saw in Tallarico the focus and professionalism that they lacked, Tallarico, while not completely sold on the pair's relatively primitive technique, was mightily impressed with the Jam Band's ragged energy, as well as a sullen, "Fuck it" attitude that Tallarico found appealing after years of playing in eager-to-please pop combos.

"I'd been playing in bands for something like seven years at this point," the singer recalled recently. "And we were always trying to get ahead, trying to rehearse and sound professional. But then I go to see the Jam Band, and it blew me away. I wasn't expecting too much. Then they got up there and did 'Rattlesnake Shake' by Fleetwood Mac. And I said to myself, 'That's it. These guys suck—they can't even tune their instruments. But they have a great groove going that's better than any fuck I've ever had.' I just knew that if I could show them a little of what I knew, with the looseness and balls that they showed up there, then we'd really have something."

The slithery blues-rock tune "Rattlesnake Shake," a consistent highlight of the Jam Band's set, was later cited by Tom Hamilton as "one of the defining songs in Aerosmith history. That song, and our version of it, sort of put together the sound that all of us love to play." ("Rattlesnake Shake" would subsequently become a recurring feature of Aerosmith's live sets; a fierce 1971 live rendition is included on *Pandora's Box*.)

Tallarico, deciding that a dose of the Jam Band's feral boogie was exactly what his stalled career needed, quickly resolved to join forces with Perry and Hamilton. At first, he intended to double on vocals and drums, replacing departing Jam Band member Pudge Scott, but soon decided that he could be of more use as a full-time frontman. In addition to deciding to bring in another member to man the skins, Tallarico suggested hiring a second guitarist to fill out the group's sound. The man he had in mind for the job was Ray Tabano, a childhood pal from Yonkers who'd been a member of his post–Chain Reaction band William Proud and who by this time had relocated to Boston, where he owned and ran a trendy leather-goods store. It was Tabano who suggested that the new band move its base of operations to Boston.

During the early stages of the newly Beantown-based (and still unnamed) band's search for a drummer, old pal Joey Kramer showed up at Tabano's leather store, seeking an audition. Born Joseph Michael Kramer in the Bronx on June 21, 1950, Joey had attended Roosevelt High School—from which he was suspended more than once for fighting—with Tallarico and Tabano, and had been drumming since the eighth grade. Since then, he'd played in an assortment of rock bands, as well as a number of black soul and R&B groups (including an early incarnation of Tavares, who in 1976 would hit the pop charts with "Heaven Must Be Missing an Angel"), wherein he'd mastered the sense of discipline and groove that would eventually emerge as a hallmark of his drumming style. Kramer was living in Boston and studying at the famed Berklee School of Music, but he was itching to get back into a rock 'n' roll band, and jumped at the chance to work with his old schoolmate Tallarico.

The feeling was mutual.

Steven Tyler, Tom Hamilton, Joe Perry, Brad Whitford, and Joey Kramer, up against the wall. (*Fin Costello/Retna*)

4

DREAM ON

"We weren't too ambitious when we started out," Steven Tyler has said. "We just wanted to be the biggest thing that ever walked the planet, the greatest rock band that ever was. We just wanted everything. We just wanted it *all.*"

If that was the case, Boston in the early seventies was a less-than-ideal location from which to launch a world-domination campaign. Musically speaking, the city was something of a ghost town, still smarting from MGM Records' disastrous late-sixties attempt to hype the more or less nonexistent "Bosstown Sound" with quickly forgotten bands like the Ultimate Spinach and the Beacon Street Union. Though there were plenty of local combos still plying their trade in local bars, their employment prospects were mainly limited to playing Top 40 covers for college students. Virtually the only homegrown bands displaying any sort of vitality or originality—or any potential for a successful recording career—were the R&B/blues-inspired J. Geils Band and the garagey Modern Lovers, neither of whom posed any immediate threat of taking the industry by storm.

"I like Boston," Tyler told *Circus* in 1974, "because it's like a city and it's not a city. New York's a little too much for me. I dig Boston because it's got Olde England in it. They've just got one big new building there. Everything else is old and rustic."

"Rustic" would be a very charitable adjective to describe the five bandmates' early experiences in their adopted hometown. For nearly two years, the five bandmates shared a squalid three-bedroom apartment on Boston's Commonwealth Avenue, barely scraping by on their meager earnings from various day jobs. (Tyler worked in a bakery for a while; Perry was a janitor in a local synagogue.)

"Times were pretty tough," Tyler recalled. "We ate a lot of brown rice back then. We managed to get a free practice room at a Boston University dorm by promising to play some dances for them. . . . They were really nice. They'd even sneak us free meals at the cafeteria when we were hard up for food."

The name Aerosmith was suggested by Kramer, who'd concocted it back in high school; the drummer's always denied that the majestic moniker had any relation to Sinclair Lewis's classic novel *Arrowsmith*. Another suggested band name was Spike Jones, in honor of the anarchic forties bandleader—that idea would have been more than a bit impractical, in light of the fact that Jones's own recordings were still on the market. Tyler, meanwhile, had suggested calling the band the Hookers, "'cause playing the clubs is prostitution anyway."

Though Tyler may have entertained visions of stardom

from the start, Perry's recollections of his original ambitions are considerably more down-to-earth. "I never envisioned what I was doing as part of a *career*," he says. "We just looked at the bands we idolized—like the Yardbirds—and we were blown away by how they could *play*. All we wanted to do was play like that, to be a great band like that."

"I think what we wanted to do, without ever really saying it, was to be the American equivalent of all the great British bands like Cream, the Yardbirds, and Led Zeppelin," adds Hamilton. "They were all so classy and powerful-sounding. We couldn't think of an American band like that. We wanted to be the first one."

And all involved agreed that this was the group to do it. "Right from the beginning," Tyler says, "there was magic in this goddamn band."

Aerosmith made its public debut in the fall of 1970 at Nimpuc Regional High School. If the venue was something less than glamorous, the set—mixing self-penned tunes from the band's growing repertoire of originals with such covers as John Lennon's "Cold Turkey," the Rolling Stones' "Live with Me," and the Yardbirds' "Shapes of Things"—was reportedly well received, even if interband relations were a tad rocky.

"Steven and Joe had an argument the first night about Joe playing too loud," Hamilton says, "and so began an Aerosmith tradition."

Early on, Aerosmith made the all-important decision to avoid the covers-oriented local club scene, in favor of venues where they could hone their original material. So it was that Aerosmith's early performances took place at a motley assortment of high-school dances, college frat parties, ski lodges, teen centers, town halls, and Navy officers' clubs, along with informal outdoor sets on the Boston University campus. That approach allowed the band to try out their originals in front of relatively enthusiastic, relatively unjaded crowds who were generally out to hear music rather than to drink or hang out.

"We never wanted to be a bar band," said Kramer. "We were always a concert band."

"We played around a lot," Perry told *Trouser Press.* "Mostly weekends, rehearsing during the week as opposed to playing in a club for a week and then being too dead to rehearse. Having to play four sets a night of other people's material really drains you. That's a trap a lot of young bands fall into—they get used to that $1,000 a week they're pulling in from playing at a club. It becomes hard for them to break out of that. You have to rehearse and you have to do new material. We avoided that trap by playing high-school dances out in the country, getting maybe $300. We had a great time then—it was a lot of fun."

Working without a manager or much of a budget, Aerosmith had to rely on its wits to survive, and the band quickly developed a knack for self-promotion, which helped spread word of the band outside of its base in the New England area. Steve Paul, who managed Johnny and Edgar Winter, and whose Scene club had been an important NYC hipster hangout in the late sixties, got wind of Aerosmith's reputation for enterprising outrageousness and offered the band an opening slot on an Edgar Winter–Humble Pie bill at New York's Academy of Music. Aerosmith's set, though plagued by sound problems, was enough to generate some all-important word of mouth in the New York area.

But a personnel change was in the cards before Aerosmith would make any further career strides. By 1971, internal disputes relating to Tabano's role in the band had grown strained beyond resolvability. After departing, the guitarist sold his leather business and disappeared to Mexico for several months. A couple of years later, he'd return to the Aerosmith organization, first as roadie and eventually as director of marketing, overseeing the band's lucrative merchandising arm. It was in the latter capacity that he would help design the band's famous winged logo.

Tabano's replacement arrived in the form of one Brad Ernest Whitford, born in Winchester, Massachusetts, on February 23, 1952. As a child, he'd studied trumpet before moving on to guitar, and began playing in an assortment of local rock bands at the age of sixteen. He'd also spent a year studying music theory and composition at Berklee, but quit when he decided that he could learn more from hands-on experience with such impressively-named local combos like the Teapot Dome, Earth Incorporated, and the Cymbals of Resistance.

When Whitford received the call from Aerosmith, he'd been playing with a fairly popular local band called Justin Tyme. Ironically, when Whitford left Justin Tyme, the group's vacant guitar slot was filled by none other than Ray Tabano, back from Mexico. The situation came full circle when Justin Tyme opened for Aerosmith not long after the two groups exchanged guitarists.

With Whitford's arrival, the final piece of Aerosmith's musical puzzle fell into place, with the new member's slashing rhythm parts providing the perfect counterbalance to Perry's electrifying leads. With Whitford on board, Aerosmith moved swiftly to consolidate the aggressive blues-based style that would subsequently form the basis for the band's later recordings—and, for that matter, much of American hard rock during the 1970s.

The combination of Tyler's strutting, insouciant vocals, Perry and Whitford's chugging tag-team axework and the steady yet inventive grooves generated by the Hamilton-Kramer rhythm section, carried a gritty integrity that made clear the band's grounding in the blues. It didn't take Aerosmith long to mine a personalized sound and a uniquely sassy attitude that transcended the group's influences.

"When you start a rock 'n' roll band, you've gotta fake it till you make it," Tyler later philosophized. "You begin by doing what you love, and what you love is usually what some other people have already done. It just depends on how much of a fool you make of yourself along the way to finding your own sound—assuming you find it."

One of Aerosmith's key inspirations—and one that would quickly become a thorn in the band's side thanks to the rock press' insistence on noting the fact—was the Rolling Stones. In a late-eighties interview with *Spin,* Perry recalled attending a Stones concert during Aerosmith's early days. "Steven and I stood on the stage at the Boston Garden after the Stones had just played there and the stage was still up. We had been playing . . . to four or five hundred, maybe a thousand. We just stood on the stage and thought, 'Well, man, someday.' In four years that was *our* stage."

By the time Whitford joined, Aerosmith was earning about $300 a night, decent-enough money for an unsigned local band during the early seventies. But, despite the group's regional popularity, its members—who by this point had quit their day jobs—were still living hand to mouth, and the group's future remained uncertain. Morale was sinking fast, but some positive changes were on the way.

John O'Toole, manager of Boston's Fenway Theater, had taken a shine to the band, and had been allowing them to use the venue as a rent-free rehearsal hall. One night, O'Toole invited Frank Connelly, one of Boston's biggest concert promoters, to come and hear them play. Almost immediately, Connelly recognized Aerosmith's potential, and offered his management services.

"Frank was the first guy who *knew*," says Whitford. "He was the one who said we were on to something."

Now installed as Aerosmith's first manager, "Father Frank" (so nicknamed for his paternal guidance) helped the band get its messy business affairs in order, and saw to it that they had a steady stream of live work. He also installed the band at the Manchester Sheraton Hotel to work up new material. For several months the five musicians resided at the hotel, rarely leaving and often jamming late into the night. By the end of the Sheraton stint, Tyler and Perry had written and demoed enough tunes for an album. But the big time still hung out of reach.

Connelly had plenty of know-how in concert booking and promotion, but possessed little experience in dealing with record companies, and knew that some high-powered contacts would be needed if Aerosmith was to score a recording deal. So he contacted Steve Leber and David Krebs, a shrewd and successful New York–based management team whose main clients at the time were the much-touted masters of pre-punk outrage, the New York Dolls. (Leber and Krebs would later add Ted Nugent, AC/DC, and the Scorpions to their roster.)

Rather than take his chances while holding on to a bigger piece of the pie, Connelly engaged Leber and

Krebs as partners in Aerosmith's management, more or less handing the group over to the pair in return for a piece of the future profits, along with a cut of the band's publishing. Leber and Krebs moved quickly to attract record-company interest, while Connelly continued to keep the fivesome busy with live gigs.

5

MAKE IT

One of Leber and Krebs' first moves as Aerosmith's new comanagers was to set up a showcase gig for the band at New York's legendary now-defunct rock 'n' roll dive, Max's Kansas City. While a representative of Atlantic Records (which had had considerable success in the booming hard-rock market with such acts as Cream, Iron Butterfly, and Led Zeppelin) opined that Aerosmith wouldn't qualify as a major label contender for at least a year, Columbia Records president Clive Davis felt no such qualms. Following the set, he appeared backstage with a simple but firm, "Yes, I think we could do something with you."

In the summer of 1972, Aerosmith signed with Columbia for a reported $125,000—not a particularly impressive sum by nineties standards, but a fairly substantial one at the time. Actually, the band was contracted to Leber and Krebs' production company, Contemporary Communications, which in turn struck a deal with Columbia to deliver Aerosmith records to the label. This convoluted arrangement—which, despite its built-in potential for financial irregularity and conflict of interest, was by no means unique in the music industry—guaranteed Leber-Krebs a hefty profit on top of their standard management percentage.

The Leber-Krebs production deal would subsequently become a bone of contention in the band's relationship with its management. But in the green and hungry days of 1972, none of this seemed relevant to the five 'Smiths, whose more immediate concerns involved ducking eviction notices and becoming famous (though not necessarily in that order), and who weren't about to look this gift horse in the mouth.

Whatever the inherent drawbacks in their new recording arrangement, it was with a distinctly charged sense of enthusiasm—and a rechristened frontman, Tallarico having adopted the less ethnic "Tyler"—that Aerosmith entered Boston's Intermedia Sound studios to record its self-titled debut album. Production chores were handled by Adrian Barber, an experienced studio hand whose résumé included work with Cream, Vanilla Fudge, the Young Rascals and the Allman Brothers Band.

With a relatively modest recording budget and recording gear that would be considered primitive by nineties standards, Barber and the band took a mere two weeks to record and mix the scrappily raucous *Aerosmith,* which, according to those who were around at the time, offers an accurate reflection of the band's then current stage act.

Though it lacks much of the compositional sophistication that the band would later bring to its work, *Aerosmith*—packaged in a self-consciously spacey sleeve picturing the band members against an ethereal (and, in original pressings, orange-tinted) sky—more than compensates with generous helpings of the straightforward ballsy "in your face"–ness and guttersnipe swagger that would soon become a band trademark. Whitford still names the embryonic debut disc as his sentimental favorite.

"That was our music," says Whitford. "The synergistic effect that the band had with each other was on that album, in songs like 'One Way Street.' We walked into the studio and they said, 'Go ahead and play your music.' All we were looking for on that track was excitement and that's exactly what we got.

"If you were to look at the equipment we recorded that album on today, you'd die laughing," Whitford notes. "I happened to look at the original board we used to record the album a while back . . . what a piece of junk! It looked like something you'd use to tune a car. But you see, it's what you get down on tape that counts."

And what the band got on tape was indeed worthy of note, a punchy—if somewhat sketchy and unfocused—blueprint for the more distinctive style that would emerge fully developed a couple of albums down the line. Seven of *Aerosmith*'s eight cuts were original compositions, with five written by Tyler alone, one by Tyler and Steven Emspack (an old roadie friend from Yonkers), and another by the soon-to-be-prolific Tyler-Perry team.

The moderately explosive "Make It" opened the album on an appropriate note of hubris, proclaiming Aerosmith's career agenda with characteristic cockiness. The second track, "Somebody," was a serviceable enough rocker whose unflatteringly thin guitar sound is briefly broken by a wordless guitar-vocal exchange that temporarily moves the song to a higher plane. Side one was closed by the seven-minute

"One Way Street," a jaunty blues strut featuring some fine harmonica by Tyler.

"Write Me a Letter" was a similarly down-and-dirty twelve-bar excursion, while "Movin' Out"—the first-ever Tyler-Perry collaboration—drew its inspiration from an eviction notice received at the band's old Commonwealth Avenue apartment. Elsewhere, the album-closing cover of Rufus Thomas's "Walkin' the Dog"—previously covered by the Rolling Stones, among others—ably demonstrated Aerosmith's innate grasp of the blues idiom as well as Tyler's talents on wood flute.

Those paragons of straight-ahead rockism were put into perspective by the seamless grandiosity of "Dream On," which boasted a gorgeously layered sound that benefitted from Adrian Barber's studio experience, alongside a yearning Tyler lyric that launched the song into a million earnest teen fantasies. With its unforced juxtaposition of lyrical sensitivity and sonic thrust, "Dream On" has been called the first power ballad—a dubious distinction perhaps, but probably an accurate one.

Aerosmith's other acknowledged classic was "Mama Kin," which encapsulated all the best qualities of the band's early rhythm 'n' roll approach, with soulful accents from sessionman David Woodford's sax.

"Mama Kin" achieved another sort of immortality when, in a burst of alcohol-fueled cockiness, Tyler celebrated the album's release by having "Makin" tattooed on his left bicep. "We thought we owned the world, and we thought 'Mama Kin' was gonna be a single," the singer later explained to *Spin.* "I walked into this tattoo parlor . . . I drew some musical notes for them, there's a G-clef in the middle, there's fire and flames . . . . It hurt like hell."

Despite Tyler's confidence, the harsh reality of record-company politics made itself apparent not long after the debut album's January 1973 release. "Aerosmith and Bruce Springsteen both put out their first records on the same day," says David Krebs, the younger half of the Leber-Krebs team, who concentrated on handling Aerosmith's affairs while partner Steve Leber attended to the New York Dolls. "And for every dollar Columbia put into Aerosmith, they put $100 into Springsteen. That was our first education."

While *Aerosmith*'s initial sales were impressive throughout most of the U.S., their hometown fans' rabid loyalty proved to be the group's saving grace. The album quickly became a top seller in the Boston area, with "Dream On" the most-requested song on most of the area's FM rock stations.

Meanwhile, the nation's rock critics began a long-running tradition of not taking Aerosmith particularly seriously. One of the few "serious" rock publications that did was the legendary Detroit magazine *Creem*, whose Dann DeWitt reviewed the debut album thusly: "*Aerosmith* is as good as coming in your pants at a drive-in at age twelve with your little sister's babysitter calling the action. . . . It's like discovering that a cherry bomb, strategically placed, can fuck up the toilets at school. . . . [The band's] format is of the classic mold: two guitars, bass, drums, a vocalist . . . but what they do out of this structure is a fucking pleasure. Sure, you'll hear influences, some quite obvious at that, but we all had to suck somebody's tit, and whatta buncha tits these chubby-lipped delinquents have gone after!"

Nonetheless, many more critics dismissed Aerosmith as cut-rate Stones imitators. The criticism plainly rankled the band, as it would continue to do for years to come, and it was often Perry who seemed to feel the sting most acutely. "We were *never* the hip band, and that was fine with us," the guitarist said recently, admitting, "All the bad press did get to be a burr in our saddles. But the truth is that fifteen thousand kids screaming for you at the Boston Garden goes a long way to making a bad review look like the piece of shit that it is."

Tyler and Perry didn't always deal with the criticism in such a philosophical manner. On a regular basis, Tyler responded defensively when critics noted Aerosmith's stylistic and attitudinal debts to the Rolling Stones, particularly when he and Perry were compared to the Stones' "Glimmer Twins," Mick Jagger and Keith Richards.

"Sure, I've been affected by Jagger. What rock singer hasn't?" Tyler griped to *Circus* in 1974. "When I go up there in front of people, I just move the way I've got to move." As for his rubber-faced mugging, Tyler commented, "I can't help it if I've got big lips."

"Look, anybody who says I'm a Jagger rip-off 'cause I look like him a little has no intelligence," the singer insisted to *Trouser Press* the following year. "Joe Perry looks like Keith Richards a little. What are we supposed to do, get plastic surgery?"

Speaking from a nineties perspective, though, Tyler would be a bit more forthright. "It sucked," he said of the charges of Stones-borrowing. "I hated it. It rubbed me the wrong way. You want to know why? Because it was true. I loved the fucking Rolling Stones. . . . Sure, the critics saw the lips and they thought Mick. That's all those beanbags wrote about us. But there was a lot more to us than that." In fairness, while Aerosmith may have modeled its bad-boy stance after the Stones', musically they owed as much to the blues-based hard-rock hybrid pioneered by the Yardbirds and Led Zeppelin.

As ego-bruising as the rock-critic establishment's neglect may have been, it was the lack of support from radio that was more practically damaging to the band's career prospects. In retrospect, it's hard to imagine now that "Dream On"—judged by rock history as a timeless masterpiece—got no higher than number 59 on the *Billboard* charts when Columbia, prodded into action by the song's phenomenal popularity in the Boston area, finally got around to releasing it as a single in June 1973.

Aerosmith's ignominious status in their record company's pecking order wasn't helped by the fact that, during the summer of 1973, Columbia was reeling from allegations of fiscal corruption that subsequently led to Clive Davis leaving the company. Not surprisingly, the label's new executive regime wasn't particularly inclined to put their energies behind the departed Davis's newest discovery.

With Columbia in temporary disarray and no assurance of radio or press support, David Krebs deemed that under the circumstances the only recourse available was to have the band tour intensively to promote the album, in an effort to conquer one regional market at a time. So Aerosmith hit the road for nearly a year, playing whatever club and college gigs they could, as well as appearing in larger venues opening for better-known bands like the Kinks and Mott the Hoople and sharing some odder bills with English space-rock kings (and fellow Leber-Krebs clients) Hawkwind.

Odder still were the dates that Aerosmith opened for guitarist John McLaughlin's prog-jazz group the Mahavishnu Orchestra, at which McLaughlin would ask for a minute of audience silence after Aerosmith's set, to "cool the vibes" before the headliners began playing. In the face of such mismatches, Aerosmith invariably came out fighting.

"It was almost like the world was asphalt and we were these fucking weeds," Tyler told *Tower Pulse* in 1993. "No matter what they put over us, asphalt or metal sealant, we grew right through it!"

Still, as a live unit Aerosmith had yet to completely get its act together. Observers noted too much awkward downtime between numbers, and front man Tyler was often less than skillful at filling the gaps. The singer now attributes those shortcomings to inexperience and—incredible as it may seem now—shyness.

"We weren't ready to become the superstars we wanted to be at the time of our first couple of albums," Perry told *Trouser Press* in 1978. "If we had known that then, it would've been a lot easier on us. We were getting upset about everything, but meantime the band wasn't hot enough to deserve better. It made us work harder."

Hard work wasn't the only habit the band picked up while touring behind its debut album. The contrast between the galvanizing buzz of performing and the stultifying boredom of between-show downtime has long driven musicians to seek distraction in alcohol and drugs, and the members of Aerosmith submitted willingly. Even at this early stage of the group's career, the members' escalating chemical intake was setting a pattern that would dog the band for years to come.

6

SAME OLD SONG AND DANCE

Though the group's first album had been a substantial success in the Boston area, and despite all the grueling roadwork they'd put in to support the album, Aerosmith was still something less than a household name in 1973. In the fall of that year, when the band entered New York's Record Plant to record its sophomore effort, *Get Your Wings,* the mood was tinged with a distinct make-or-break vibe.

Handling production chores this time around were Jack Douglas and Ray Colcord. Earning "executive producer" credit was occasional studio visitor Bob Ezrin, who'd won fame as producer of Alice Cooper's influential early-seventies albums *Love It to Death, Killer, School's Out* and *Billion Dollar Babies,* as well as overseeing the New York Dolls' self-titled 1973 debut effort.

Steven Tyler tends to the unique demands of his stage regalia.
(*Scott Weiner/Retna*)

While Ezrin possessed the bigger name, it was Jack Douglas (who'd engineered the aforementioned Dolls LP) who would ultimately have a long-term influence on Aerosmith's career, quickly establishing himself as a crucial member of the band's creative team. From the beginning, Douglas and the group shared an enormous personal rapport and creative chemistry, and the band members have always been quick to credit Douglas's contributions in their creative process.

Douglas, according to Whitford, quickly became "like our sixth member. We did everything together. In the studio he was open to anything, always willing to experiment." His skills as an arranger and technician were crucial in translating Aerosmith's roguish, hard-headed essence to the recording medium, and the progress evident in the grooves of *Get Your Wings* made it clear just how much Douglas brought to the table.

The album (one of whose working titles, interestingly enough, was *Night in the Ruts*), showed the group making some significant creative strides, with a more cohesive band sound and a set of lyrics carrying a more distinctive Aerosmith character. The album's leadoff track (and first single), the gloriously slinky Tyler-Perry composition "Same Old Song and Dance," humorously related its shaggy-dog tale of sleaze and degradation, while adding a swaggering four-man horn section (including Elephant's Memory member Stan Bronstein and session aces the Brecker Brothers) to the mix.

A similarly sassy tone infused "S.O.S. (Too Bad)," the title being a pissed-off acronym for "same old shit." "Woman of the World," meanwhile, was a somewhat routine holdover from Tyler's Chain Reaction days. "Spaced," the album's other Tyler-Perry composition, remains one of the more out-of-character items in the Aerosmith catalogue, a post-apocalyptic sci-fi tale whose vaguely futuristic story-line was blunted by a musical execution that wasn't quite up to the challenge of the song's lyrical pretensions.

But it was the spookily evocative acoustic-based ballad "Seasons of Wither"—inspired by a particularly bleak home-bound autumn evening—that was the album's biggest wild card, its pensive (and surprisingly mature) introspection providing a nice contrast to the randier fare that dominated the early Aerosmith repertoire. Recalling the song's origins, Tyler relates, "You know what Tuinals and Seconal are? Well, I was eating those at the time, big time. I was living with Joey Kramer near a chicken farm. It was Halloween and I was really down. So I went down to the basement, burned some incense, and picked up this guitar that Joey had found in a Dumpster somewhere. It was fretted pretty fucked, and it had a special tone to it. I love that song."

The vaguely uneasy album-closer "Pandora's Box," a rare Tyler-Kramer collaboration, was inspired by the same beat-up guitar. "We were rehearsing up in New Hampshire, and I was living in Vermont," Kramer recalled of his first-ever writing credit. "I came up with the riff on that [guitar]. I played it for Steven, and he went to work."

While recording in Manhattan, the band stayed at the Ramada Inn on Forty-eighth Street and Eighth Avenue. Some of that neighborhood's more unsavory inhabitants provided inspiration for the tongue-in-cheek lyrics of the cheerfully sleazy "Lord of the Thighs," which stood as the first definitive demonstration of Tyler's unparalleled knack for lascivious lyrical innuendo.

Hamilton recalls the song's musical origins: "I remember we needed one more song for *Get Your Wings* and we needed it fast. We locked ourselves into Studio C at the Record Plant for the night. And ['Lord of the Thighs'] is what we came up with. I remember Steven was really psyched and I think that it shows."

"Was I the Lord of the Thighs? Fuck yeah," says Tyler.

Ironically, though, *Get Your Wings'* most quintessentially Aerosmithian tune is the album's lone cover, "Train Kept A Rollin'," originally popularized in the mid-fifties by rockabilly star Johnny Burnette and his Rock 'n' Roll Trio, although Aerosmith patterned their rendition—a studio recording, despite the overdubbed crowd noises—after the frenetic arrangement recorded by their heroes the Yardbirds a decade later.

"All of us loved the Yardbirds' version," says Perry. "We all knew it and had played it before we got together. Our version was pretty sterile on the album, but it was a great song for us to play [live], more our kind of thing than something like 'Roll Over Beethoven.'"

That "Train Kept A Rollin'" was released as *Get Your Wings'* second single and remained Aerosmith's standard setcloser for several years to come is interesting in light of longstanding rumors that the album version's crackling axework may have been by Alice Cooper sidemen Steve Hunter and Dick Wagner.

Get Your Wings amply demonstrated Aerosmith's musical and compositional progress, but upon its March 1974 release the album failed to achieve the decisive commercial breakthrough that the band was looking for. Still, there were plenty of encouraging signs, and some distinct evidence that the band's grass-roots-level work in support of the first album had not been in vain. It shouldn't have been surprising when *Get Your Wings* became the top-selling album in the Boston area within a few weeks of its release; it was rather more noteworthy that "Same Old Song and Dance" became a substantial FM-airplay hit nationally when released as the album's first single.

In the wake of *Get Your Wings'* release, Aerosmith once again hit the road with a vengeance, supporting English heavy-metal kingpins Black Sabbath and Deep Purple while headlining their own shows in their New England stronghold. The punishing pace of the band's roadwork was beginning to pay off in the increasing style and assurance of its stage show, which saw the instrumental team clicking into a new level of rapport and Tyler coming into his own as a performer, developing a distinctive visual style highlighted by his gawkily graceful stage moves and flamboyant stage outfits.

Addressing the origins of his trademark scarf-wrapped-around-the-mike-stand, Tyler spilled the beans to *Hit Parader*: "I usually don't answer that. I don't know, I had a scarf on once, I wrapped it around there, and it looked good. It's nice to hide behind, whip it around . . ." Many of Tyler's stage scarves contained secret compartments in which the singer hid the non-prescription pills that were becoming an increasingly integral element of his life.

In a pronouncement that would take on increased portent in light of subsequent events, Tyler told *Circus,* "Look, I can't tell kids to take or not take drugs. I feel too much like one of them. I'm not really any different."

Though not an instant smash, *Get Your Wings*—which in keeping with its title featured a primitive version of the band's soon-to-be-ubiquitous "winged" logo on its cover—benefited from the band's diligent promotion efforts. The album lingered stubbornly around the middle of the charts for more than a year, steadily selling an unspectacular but respectable 5–6,000 copies a week; it would finally go gold early in 1975.

Reviewing the album in the *Village Voice*, Robert Christgau referred to Aerosmith as "musicianly (all things are relative) inheritors of the Grand Funk principle: if a band is going to be dumb, it might as well be American dumb. Here they're loud and cunning enough to provide a real treat for the hearing-impaired, at least on side one. Have a sense of humor about themselves, too, assuming 'Lord of the Thighs' is intended as a joke. With dumb bands, it's always hard to tell."

Christgau's backhanded acclaim was symptomatic of the grudging appreciation that Aerosmith received even from the critics who *liked* the band, and the lack of respect still rubbed the 'Smiths the wrong way. That frustration sometimes manifested itself in the band members' resentment of the media attention commanded by their Leber-Krebs stablemates the New York Dolls, who in their 1973–74 heyday had little commercial success but plenty of hip cachet. Alone among his bandmates, Joe Perry had an instinctive appreciation for the Dolls' passionately outrageous, intentionally amateurish glitter-punk.

"I used to see them every chance I'd get," Perry told *Trouser Press* in 1978. "I remember the first time I saw them at the Mercer Arts Center—it was just after we'd signed with Leber-Krebs. I thought they were the best band in the world, although it took a couple of minutes to get my ears adjusted to the fact that they were out of tune most of the time. The rest of the guys in Aerosmith hated them."

It's ironic, then, in light of this rather petty rivalry, that Steven Tyler eventually married Cyrinda Fox, ex-wife of Dolls frontman David Johansen. That's rock 'n' roll. . . .

7

WALK THIS WAY

Aerosmith first appeared at a stage of rock history when the last gasps of sixties musical idealism were about to mutate into the full-on decadence of commercial seventies rock. The times seemed to call for a band that could bridge the gap between sixties roots and seventies hedonism, and in 1975 Aerosmith was on the verge of demonstrating that it possessed the qualities to occupy that niche.

In the early months of 1975, Aerosmith returned to the Record Plant, this time with Jack Douglas taking the reins as sole producer. *Toys in the Attic,* the album that would emerge from those sessions, was the one that would cement Aerosmith's growing reputation as a world-class act, showcasing a tightly-wound, newly focused musical attack—and selling more than five million copies in the process. Brad Whitford described the experience of making *Toys in the Attic* as "everything clicking into place."

By far the band's most accomplished effort yet, *Toys in the Attic* was where Aerosmith *really* got its wings. "The band this time around is more versatile," Steven Tyler told *Circus* upon the album's release. "That's what I always admired about the Beatles. They'd come out and do 'Sexy Sadie' and then go into 'Helter Skelter.' That's the kind of thing I'd like to do—four or five rockers and then go into a ballad that takes you to another land and then back into another gasser. That's what this new album's about."

Toys in the Attic was also the first Aerosmith album to truly capture the full burn of Aerosmith's live concerts. And nowhere was that incendiary energy better demonstrated than on the album's aggressively infectious title track, written by the increasingly formidable Tyler-Perry team, which stood as the band's most accomplished anthem yet. Joe Perry described it as "a benchmark rock 'n' roll song for Aerosmith—that kind of fast tune that was always a favorite of mine. [That] was sort of the first one. There were many more to follow."

Less well-known, but equally worthy of note, were the crunchingly metallic "Round and Round," which marked Brad Whitford's first songwriting credit, and the winning piano-driven ballad "You See Me Crying," another old Chain Reaction tune, featuring a particulary affecting Tyler vocal. By contrast, the rather bathetic "Uncle Salty" (on which cowriter Tom Hamilton played rhythm guitar) was a well-intentioned but ultimately unsuccessful attempt at bittersweet relevance, relating the tale of a young girl's descent into drugs and prostitution.

For the most part, though, *Toys in the Attic* found Aerosmith sticking to what it knew best, as demonstrated by the eloquently naughty "Adam's Apple," which found Tyler (who again wrote or cowrote all eight of the album's original tunes) in typically randy form. "That's Steven," Perry laughed in acknowledgment of his bandmate's lyrical preoccupation with sex. "He hasn't changed anything but his clothes since we started the band."

"Sweet Emotion," which was released as the album's first single in April, was a bracingly lustful epic, originally inspired by the sight of a teen nymphette baring her flesh at an Aerosmith show, with some typically tart Tyler wordplay and Hamilton-penned music that combined a vaguely Eastern atmosphere with all-American boogie. The song initially grew out of Hamilton's bass noodling into one of the band's most ambitious arrangements.

The tune, according to Hamilton, "came at the very end of the *Toys in the Attic* sessions. I had my part, but I was too shy to say, 'Hey, let's work on it.' But somehow we had an extra day at the end, and Jack said, 'Anyone have anything we can jam on?' And so this one made it at the last minute. I remember showing Steven this riff a couple of times during the *Get Your Wings* sessions and he just didn't like it. My immediate reaction was just to forget it. But one day we started the riff at a different point, and it shed a whole new light on it."

As for the song's slyly enigmatic lyrics, Tyler explains. "A lot of stuff I wrote in the old days just came out of anger. 'Sweet Emotion' was about how pissed off I was at Joe's ex-wife, and all the other frustrations of the time. I could never get through to him."

But the album's defining song was the riveting "Walk This Way," which wedded an insistent Perry guitar riff with a typically suggestive teen sex lyric. Tyler told

Raw magazine, "That song started as just a Joe Perry lick, and then I put my rhythmic lyrics that stem from my days as a drummer on top of that. I remember making up those lyrics the night we were meant to record the vocals. I wrote them on the walls of the Record Plant stairway. When I listen to that song now, it's so raw you can tell I wrote those lyrics on the spot."

Hamilton later revealed that "Walk This Way"'s inspiration came partially from a decidedly unlikely source: "We were rehearsing that riff, and I don't think Steven was even around that day as we practiced it and arranged it. And that night we went with Jack Douglas to the movies and saw *Young Frankenstein*. There's that part in the movie where Igor says, 'Walk this way,' and the other guy walks the same way with the hump and everything. We thought it was the funniest thing we'd ever seen in our lives. So we told Steven the name of this song has got to be 'Walk This Way,' and he took it from there."

But Tyler's affinity for lyrical innuendo, previously demonstrated on "Lord of the Thighs" and "Pandora's Box," was matched by the album's one non-original, a swingingly upbeat revival of the risqué 1952 novelty tune "Big Ten-Inch Record," with sessionman Scott Cushnie providing hard-stomping honky-tonk piano and Tyler blowing some mean harmonica. Tyler had heard the original version of the song on a tape of DJ Dr. Demento's syndicated radio show.

In contrast to the album's general tone of good-natured leering was the lyrical revelation of the memorably jangly "No More No More," whose lyrics gave some hint of the increasing psychic toll taken by the band's punishing studio-tour cycle and the chemical adventures that were becoming a growing force in the five musicians' lives. "Blood stains the ivories of my daddy's baby grand/Ain't seen the daylight since we started this band," Tyler sang, adding, "If I don't start changing, I'll be writing my will."

"I still love [that] song because of Steven's lyrics," Perry stated in the 1990s. "It's not one of those stupid, generic 'I love rock 'n' roll' songs that some bands do. It's a real song about the rock 'n' roll lifestyle, or *our* rock 'n' roll lifestyle. I don't know if it's the definitive song about life on the road, and I don't even care. It's like a page from our diary."

Even *Toys in the Attic*'s cover art, which depicted an attic full of neglected playthings clamoring for their young owner's attention, carried particular thematic resonance. Speaking with *Circus,* Tyler described an earlier, rejected version of the cover: "All the toys were standing around looking at this teddy bear sitting in the middle with his wrist slit and stuffing all over the floor. That was the original concept, but that was getting a little too off-the-wall even for Humpty Dumpty, so we decided to take the other route where it's a kind of fantasy where the toys are up in the attic wondering when the kids who used to play with them would come back."

Alongside the band's ever-evolving compositional skills, *Toys in the Attic* showcased Perry's growth as a distinctive guitarist with a knack for combining aggression and invention.

In an all-too-rare instance of cultural synchronicity, Aerosmith's emergence as a musical force coincided with its commercial breakthrough. Immediately upon its release in April 1975, *Toys in the Attic* broke into the Top 20, reaching gold-record status by the end of the summer and platinum by the end of the year. As 1976 dawned, Aerosmith was firmly established as Columbia's biggest-selling act—bigger than Bruce Springsteen, bigger than Bob Dylan, bigger even than Barbra Streisand.

In addition to receiving increased support from album-rock (AOR) radio, *Toys in the Attic* even saw Aerosmith gain some unexpected exposure on AM Top 40 stations, thanks to the single release of the irresistible boogie "Walk This Way" and the less distinctive but undeniably appealing "You See Me Crying." In December, the now three-year-old "Dream On" was reissued once again at Krebs' prompting, finally giving the band its first Top 10 single and becoming the ubiquitous anthem it always seemed destined to become.

In the nineties, Tyler, sole author of "Dream On," attempted to shed some light on the song's enduring appeal: "For me this song sums up the shit you put up with when you're in a new band. Only one in fifty people who write about you pick up on the music. Most of the critics panned our first album, and said we were ripping off the Stones. And I think 'Dream On' is a great song, but it was two or three years before people really got a chance to hear it. That's a good barometer of my anger at the press, which I still have. 'Dream On' came of me playing the piano when I was about seventeen or eighteen, and I didn't know anything about writing a song. It was just this little . . . sonnet that I started playing one day. I never thought then it would end up being a real song or anything."

Even the more skeptical critics had to note the progress apparent on *Toys in the Attic*. "These boys are learning a trade in record time—even the sludgy numbers get crazy," Robert Christgau wrote in the *Village Voice*. "Tyler has a gift for the dirty line as well as the dirty look—anybody who can hook a song called 'Adam's Apple' around the phrase 'love at first bite' deserves to rehabilitate a blue blues like 'Big Ten-Inch Record.'"

Writing about the band in *Creem,* Wayne Robins saw in Aerosmith's surging popularity a backlash against the glitter-rock androgyny that was briefly in vogue during the early seventies. "Coming after a brief era when rock 'n' roll fans in their adolescence were bombarded with the exaggerated sexual ambiguity of Alice, Bowie, and [Lou] Reed," Robins offered, "it must be reassuring to have a band that knows everything we've wanted to know about sex all along: that it's dirty."

Indeed, Aerosmith was clearly emerging as America's classiest, most articulate exponent of the decadent spirit that would dominate mainstream American hard rock for much of the 1970s. But, despite having some musical and visual elements in common with the short-lived glitter craze, Aerosmith was fundamentally a straight-on rock band at heart.

"Our emphasis is on the music, not the clothes we wear," Kramer told *Rock* magazine. "We don't substitute gimmicks for being able to play."

In an era when arena-level rock bands were learning to fall back on elaborate staging and visual gimmickry as a substitute for musical skill, Aerosmith prided itself on delivering the goods in concert. "I've been going to a lot of concerts lately," Tyler told *Rolling Stone,* "watching groups who're so fucking outrageous on record that you'd think they'd get out there onstage and shake ass. But they just stand there. The songs we write aren't the kind that you can come out and fucking genuflect. We play kick-ass music."

Despite *Toys in the Attic*'s overall success, Aerosmith's appeal still varied in different parts of the U.S. While they were headlining heroes in their hometown and various eastern cities, they were stll considerably less than huge in the South and on the West Coast.

"I'll tell you why," Perry complained to *Creem,* addressing the regional nature of the band's popularity. "No press. No airplay. No single. No support, really, from the record company. In L.A., it's just the name on the marquee at the Whisky—below somebody else. The only reason we've gotten anywhere in Detroit is that we [played there] third on the bill a couple of times, then second."

Yet for all of his carping about those in the industry and the media who were supposedly bent on impeding Aerosmith's progress, Joe Perry often seemed to long for their respect and acknowledgment, as if he privately doubted that he and his band were truly worthy of their present success.

"Before, it was a struggle to keep alive. Now it's more of a struggle to find a sound," he told *Rock* magazine. "We can keep playing the largest arenas in the country, but we'd never be answering that question of our basic value. Our biggest struggle now is to make an artistic dent. General Motors makes a lot of money but doesn't have respect from people who know cars."

"Oftentimes I wonder if I'm doing it right," Perry confessed in *Creem.* "If I'm actually contributing. Are we doing something good, or are we just followers? . . . That's the truth, I don't know. . . . To satisfy my own artistic needs, I wonder if the things I write . . . maybe I'm *not* getting better on guitar. Maybe I'm *not* better than your average guitar player. But I'll tell ya. If I find out after a year or so more that I'm not improving, I'll just quit touring and work on my cars."

Aerosmith was already well into a typically intensive tour schedule by the time *Toys in the Attic* hit the racks. With Scott

Cushnie filling out the sound on keyboards, the tour found the group easing comfortably into its new status as arena headliner, while adding new fuel to the band's growing notoriety as a three-ring circus of contentious behavior.

In June, Tyler managed to get himself arrested after he and Kramer staged an impromptu pre–Fourth of July fireworks display from Tyler's hotel window in Lincoln, Nebraska. In September, a *Rolling Stone* story caught the ever-mercurial Tyler, minutes before Aerosmith was due to open for ZZ Top at a Los Angeles arena, threatening not to go onstage if a minor equipment problem was not sorted out. At a subsequent San Diego show, the singer was seen smashing the band's entire backstage buffet table over some now-forgotten dispute.

Then there was the time in Memphis when Tyler was dragged off by the local constabulary for saying "fuck" onstage. "They were planning on coming onstage and taking me off," Tyler recounted. "So our road manager talked to the policemen and said, 'Let 'em finish off the set and then take him off to jail.' Meanwhile, one of our roadies told me what was going down. So I went over to the lighting guy and said, 'As soon as the show's over, I want you to black out the house.' I finished up 'Train Kept A Rollin',' jumped into the audience and ran up the aisle. But just as I reached the lobby, police surrounded me with guns drawn, shouting, 'Hold it!' They handcuffed me."

An all-too-rare instance of restraint playing a role in Aerosmith's affairs.

Even at his drug-addled worst, Tyler always knew how to make an entrance. (*Fin Costello/Retna*)

8

BACK IN THE SADDLE

Toys in the Attic had solidly established Aerosmith's credentials as American hard rock's new standard-bearers, combining ballsiness, accessibility and cheerfully sleazy humor with a lyrical intelligence and stylistic flair that showed the band to be miles ahead of most of its contemporaries, but still reliably down-to-earth.

"We were America's band," reflects Joe Perry. "We were the garage band that made it really big—the ultimate party band. We were the guys who you could actually see. Back then in the seventies, it wasn't like Led Zeppelin was out there on the road in America all of the time. The Stones weren't always coming to your town. We were. You could count on us to come by."

Indeed, by the middle of the decade the Rolling Stones and Led Zeppelin were firmly entrenched as exalted rock royalty, while the earthier Aerosmith seemed more like the "good bad but not evil" boys next door, their philosophical agenda reflecting the hard-partying concerns of most of their audience.

As Charles M. Young would later observe in *Musician,* "In the mid-seventies, Led Zeppelin stood on the cusp of metal and hard rock, dominating both fields as the Yankees once dominated baseball. Zeppelin had created so much money and turmoil, however, that they weren't touring that much. In the age of disco and punk, who would gather the tribe of American hard-rock fans in football stadiums when Zeppelin was grounded? There were three: Kiss, ZZ Top, and Aerosmith. The subject of screaming features in every issue of *Circus* and only the occasional grudging nod from the more respectable journals of popular culture, they appealed to the younger siblings of the Vietnam generation."

The members of Aerosmith came to refer to their fans by the affectionate collective nickname "the Blue Army." "We'd look out into the crowd when we were onstage," Tom Hamilton explains, "and all we could see was what looked like millions of guys in blue jeans. It was just like this huge sea of blue."

Energized by *Toys in the Attic*'s decisive success, the band plunged into the making of its fourth album—working at the Record Plant with Jack Douglas again—with renewed vigor. But the goods proved a bit more elusive this time around, thanks to Tyler's struggle to deliver an album's worth of lyrics. At one point, the band joked about titling the new album *Aerosmith Five* in honor of all the unused instrumental tracks they'd recorded while waiting for Tyler's contributions.

"Too much road, I guess," Brad Whitford said at the time, attempting to explain the delays in the album's completion. "It's really Steven's problem since he writes the lyrics. You get on the road and you're just cut away from reality. . . . You can only write so much about the road, and Steven is a story-teller really. You come off the road and your brain is empty."

In fact, the delays were a direct reflection of the band members' rapidly escalating drug use. Perry first began shooting heroin during the *Rocks* sessions, while Tyler—who'd moved swiftly up the pharmaceutical ladder from pot, barbiturates, co-caine, Tuinals, Seconals and LSD—was already a regular user. The other three 'Smiths dabbled in various drugs to varying de-grees, but at this point they still tended more toward heavy drinking.

Still, the extended gestation period yielded a classic album, one that many of the group's staunchest admirers still consider to be *the* essential Aerosmith release, the bluntly (and appropriately) titled *Rocks*.

The album's contents bear out its reputation. Behind its pointedly direct cover art, featuring five matched diamonds against a stark black background, lurked nine lovingly mined musical gems that showed the band sharpening its trademark blend of meat-and-potatoes rock and crafty melodic sophistica-tion. It's generally agreed that *Rocks* represents Aerosmith's sev-enties musical peak, demonstrating both the band's respect for its musical roots and its ability to transcend them to produce personal, distinctive rock 'n' roll. Douglas's smart production smoothed out some of the band's rougher edges without dulling the ferocious aggression of the band's prior work.

The bracingly cocky "Back in the Saddle," which would open the band's live sets for years to come, launched the al-bum in startling style, followed up by "Last Child," a picturesque fantasy reportedly inspired by Tyler's experiences as a youth in the rural environs of Sunapee. "Rats in the Cellar," wedded a pummeling Tyler-Perry tune to Tyler's lyrical reminiscences about his down-and-out early days in New York City—complete with banjo from session player Paul Prestopino and some guitar riffs borrowed from "Rattlesnake Shake," the Fleetwood Mac blues tune that had so impressed Tyler the first time he saw the Jam Band play in Sunapee. "We needed an answer to 'Toys in the Attic,'" said Perry. "We were getting lower and more down and dirty. So the cellar seemed like a good place to go."

The insistently groove-intensive "Combination," notable as Joe Perry's first solo composition, found its author sharing the vocal spotlight with Tyler. The rumbling "Nobody's Fault," driven by Joey Kramer's shuffle-beat and Perry's imposing wah-wah lines, with a ruefully humorous lyric was inspired by California's earthquake problems. "Get the Lead Out" was a satisfyingly sleazy slice of Tyler-Perry funk-junk, while "Lick and a Promise" was a convincing anthem of degradation, and the poignant album-closer "Home Tonight" caught Tyler (acquitting himself quite nicely on piano) in an uncharacteristically sentimental mood, with the band backed by a 101-piece orchestra and Perry offering one of his most heartfelt solos yet.

Elsewhere, the band reshuffled its instrumental lineup for the Hamilton-penned "Sick As a Dog." "Tom wrote the song on guitar, so when we recorded it I played bass and he played guitar along with Brad," Perry explained. "I was in the control room so that I could hear what I was playing on bass better, but when it came to the solo at the end, I gave the bass to Steven, ran out of the control room and picked up a guitar. For the end part, there are three guitars and Steven playing bass. We did it three or four times, the whole routine, until we got a good take. . . . We could have done it a lot easier by overdubbing. It wouldn't have had the same feel, though."

"Actually we're getting to where we should be," Perry noted in *Creem*. "The songwriting is pretty well divided up among everybody in the band, and nobody but members of the band play on this record, which is how it should be. When we started together, the idea was that everybody contributed and nobody outside did anything.

"Jack [Douglas] is really a member of the group by now," Perry continued. "He started with us, and he's grown as we have. With *Toys in the Attic* both Jack and the rest of the band sort of simultaneously found our groove. I can't imagine using another producer."

By now, Aerosmith's mainstream popularity was such that *Rocks* went platinum immediately upon release. (It would go on to sell more than three times that amount.) The quintet had also risen to new heights as one of the top-grossing acts in the U.S. concert market, occupying the same platinum-level stratosphere inhabited by the likes of Led Zeppelin, Alice Cooper, Jethro Tull, and Rod Stewart and the Faces.

To support *Rocks,* Aerosmith spent two and a half months playing headlining shows in 10,000-plus capacity arenas and larger outdoor stadiums. Perry expressed regret over playing huge stadium shows, but acknowledged the practical realities of the band's situation. "What can you do? You can't play a theater for five weeks. We tried it in Boston, we held off going into the Garden and did three nights at the Music Hall, to accommodate all the people. It's getting so that for 60,000 people to see you, if you did 5,000-seat halls, you'd be on the road for two years."

Still, the guitarist prided himself on the continuing energy and spontaneity of Aerosmith's live show.

"I could go out and play licks from the album," he told *Trouser Press,* "but where's the fun? Where's the sport? For the band to go out and do exactly the same stuff every night is boring—it's a cop-out to do just what's on the album. If you fuck around, sometimes you have genius nights, sometimes you have shit nights. . . . My sense of humor gets out of hand sometimes, which really bugs the hell out of Steven. He'd like me to play straight-ahead rhythms, but I like to make a lot of noise and shit."

The *Rocks* tour gave Aerosmith its first opportunity to headline New York's Madison Square Garden, where they had played the previous year as openers for Black Sabbath. Meanwhile, tickets for Aerosmith's headlining show at the 80,000-seat Dome Stadium in Pontiac, Michigan—the band's biggest show to date, and duly recorded for possible album release—sold out the day they went on sale.

During the *Rocks* tour, Aerosmith played several dates with the Jeff Beck–Jan Hammer band as its opening act, giving Perry the opportunity to spend time with his personal guitar idol, ex-Yardbird Beck. "It was like watching a guitar lesson every night," Perry enthused. "Imagine Brad and me going out there and watching this insanity go on, and then having to follow it. To me it wasn't headlining, it was following." At one California show, Beck jammed with Aerosmith on "Train Kept a Rollin'" and "I Ain't Got You," the two Yardbirds covers in the Aerosmith catalogue.

Despite the band's upwardly-spiraling commercial fortunes, Aerosmith continued to be plagued by an increasing tangle of interpersonal traumas, many of them stemming from the naturally volatile and contradictory personality of Steven

Tyler, whose natural quirks were increasingly intensified by his escalating drug use.

Perry was forthright about the band's fundamental instability. "Ever since we started this band, people said it'll last a month or two weeks," he told *Rock* magazine. "We have arguments. Nobody gets along. After a while we have it out. The fact that we do, though, means that the next day we can look each other in the eye. A lot of groups would hold it in and break up."

In an interview with *Rock* magazine, Joey Kramer put a positive spin on Aerosmith's combustible internal chemistry. "If we've handled it up until now, we can do anything," the drummer stated. "I think we've already come and gone from any point of breaking up. We've been to where you're just holding the other guy's shirt with your fist back like this and doing everything but fucking connecting with the nose. . . . Steve's really funny. Like, he's got three or four grand tied up in a stereo system with four-track recorders in his living room. But just go into his bedroom and he sleeps on the floor on a pillow. He doesn't have a bed!" Kramer eventually gave Tyler a bed as a gift.

Meanwhile, colorful tales of Tyler's mercurial behavior were showing up with increasing frequency in the rock press' coverage of the band's exploits, which goes a long way toward explaining the Aerosmith organization's increasing wariness—often verging on proprietary paranoia—in media matters. In the spring of 1976, for example, a writer for *Rock* magazine showed up for an interview in Tyler's L.A. hotel room to find the singer on the phone in a frantic exchange with a friend in Boston who'd informed Tyler that his apartment had just been burglarized.

"I'm going to get on a plane and blow these

gigs, man," Tyler threatened. "I'm going to find out if it's the FBI. Because I talk about coke and all kinds of bull-shit on the phone. . . ." During the same interview, the writer noted a "formidable stash of fireworks" sharing trunk space with Tyler's silk stage outfits.

Journalist Dave Hickey, working on an Aerosmith feature for *Creem,* was handed a battery of half-baked excuses for repeatedly being denied an audience with Tyler. Coincidentally, the day after Tyler failed to show up for a scheduled interview with Hickey, the writer happened to mention the fact to an artist he was interviewing for another story.

"Oh, I can tell you why," the unidentified performer said, " 'Cause Steven was out here fucking around with me all afternoon." And what's he like? Hickey asked. "Crazed. He's suddenly got all this money flying in the windows and doors and he doesn't know how to cope with it. Steven's suddenly decided that he's evil." And is he? Hickey asked. "No, I'm afraid not. He's just another rocker."

Aerosmith's chemical intake had reached such worrying levels that Leber-Krebs discouraged the group from touring overseas, for fear that customs officers would nab them carrying contraband. Eventually, though, in late 1976 the band braved the risk of a border bust to undertake its first assault on Britain and the European continent, where they had thus far failed to gain a commercial foothold.

CBS Records' London office felt particular pressure to give Aerosmith a successful U.K. launch, in light of the label's disastrous hype the previous year in conjunction with Bruce Springsteen's first visit to Britain. Hawkwind manager Doug Smith, engaged by Leber-Krebs as Aerosmith's U.K. management representative, pulled off a left-field publicity coup by getting the band's name printed on the trunks of one of the partici-pants in an important, internationally televised boxing match.

Other publicity schemes were somewhat less successful, however—thanks to Tyler's unpredictability and the growing fortress mentality within the band's inner circle. High-powered English publicist Richard Ogden, hired to maximize media awareness of the tour, brought journalist Chris Welch, from the influential British music weekly *Melody Maker,* to Tyler's New Hampshire estate to interview the vocalist. Ogden and Welch ended up spending two days in the singer's mansion waiting for Tyler—who was hiding out in an empty building nearby—to make himself available for an interview. Once Tyler finally showed up, Welch was treated to a white-knuckle spin in the singer's Porsche, a dizzying speedboat ride across Lake Sunapee, and a guided tour of Tyler's large gun collection. Un-fortunately, the veteran journalist incurred the rock star's dis-pleasure when he declined to share the lines of cocaine that Tyler snorted throughout the interview.

The European tour was pervaded by a similar blend of surreal comedy and vague menace. When the trek kicked off in mid-October with shows in Liverpool, Glasgow, Birmingham, and London, the band found itself slagged mercilessly by the ever-acerbic British music press. Meanwhile, Tyler threw one of his fabled temper tantrums backstage after a show at London's Hammersmith Odeon, following a fight with his then paramour, former *Playboy* centerfold and legendary "girlfriend to the stars" Bebe Buell. After impulsively smashing the backstage buf-fet, Tyler was spotted on his knees attempting to clean up the mess.

That outburst, while amusing in its utter strange-ness, was one more example of Tyler's increasingly bizarre behavior, which was earning him plenty of unwanted notoriety as a demanding rock-star type with a distinctly short fuse. As Tyler's chemical dependency manifested itself in increasingly severe mood swings, Aerosmith's reputation for excess and unreliablity grew.

The tour proved to be a substantial money-loser, thanks to such extravagances as the rented 45-seat private plane in which the band traveled to gigs. The plane reportedly cost the band 18,000 British pounds a night, while their shows were only bringing in a paltry 2,000 or 3,000 pounds each (approximately one-tenth of what the band would earn for their Stateside concerts). Meanwhile, the tour's value as a publicity tool was undercut by the band's habit of blowing off interviews, all the better to alienate the already skeptical British music press.

The sting of the European debacle, though, was eased by the band's continuing success in their homeland, where the *Toys in the Attic* track "Walk This Way"—which Krebs had convinced Columbia to reissue as a single—became a Top Ten hit as 1977 dawned.

In his mostly positive *Village Voice* review of *Rocks,* Robert Christgau observed, "They've retooled Led Zeppelin till the English warhorse is all glitz and flow, beating the shit out of Boston and Ted Nugent and Blue Oyster Cult in the process. . . . A warning, though: Zep's fourth represented a songmaking peak, before the band began to outgrow itself, and the same may prove true for this lesser group, so get it while you can."

That warning would prove all too prophetic.

In case anyone was wondering, Aerosmith were very big in the 1970s. (*Fin Costello/Retna*)

9

S.O.S.

Although the disastrous European trek had understandably intensified Aerosmith's disinclination to take on overseas markets, the group was already committed to undertaking its first tour of Japan beginning in early 1977. No one was particularly surprised that the quintet approached its first visit to the Far East with the sort of reckless disregard of consequences that was quickly becoming an Aerosmith trademark.

The tour began on a sour—and characteristically twisted—note. The first show, on January 29 at Maebashi, found the band trashing its backstage area after deciding that the turkey commanded by the band's contract rider—which had to be imported at considerable expense by the show's promoter—wasn't up to their standards.

By Japanese standards of decorum, the turkey incident

was a severe-enough breach of etiquette to cause concern that the rest of the tour might be cancelled. While the band managed to finish the remaining Nippon dates without any major international incidents, it would be several years before Aerosmith would be invited back to the Land of the Rising Sun.

Meanwhile, back in the States, Aerosmith's popularity was still reaching new peaks. The next obvious move might have been to take advantage of the momentum by recording a new album as quickly as possible. David Krebs, however, must have realized that, due to the severity of various members' chemical problems and the toll taken by the constant roadwork, any immediate attempt to squeeze more eggs out of this solid-gold goose could push the increasingly fragile band irretrievably over the edge.

So it was that Aerosmith was allowed its first extended break from musical activity since the beginning of its recording career. For much of the first part of 1977, the exhausted musicians had the rare opportunity to enjoy the mansions, sports cars, private planes, and home recording gear that they'd accumulated as the spoils of their commercial successes.

"If I had the same amount of money and I could stay at home, I wouldn't be bored," Joe Perry had earlier told *Hit Parader,* during one of the band's marathon tours. "The traveling is a drag, you have to get up every morning . . . it's terrible, you have to face that every day. I'd rather be home. I have four cars at home, you know how many miles I'll put on my cars this year? Nothing. I've got a couple of Porsches . . . a Turbo . . . I've got a Corvette . . . I never get to drive them. When I get home I try and drag all the kids that I can, they don't know who I am. . . ."

Perry used some of his time away from Aerosmith to

open his 16-track home studio to David Johansen—former front man of the now defunct New York Dolls—who was beginning work on his self-titled debut solo album. Perry was originally planning to coproduce the album with Jack Douglas, but the pair's Aerosmith commitments, combined with other distractions, kept that plan from reaching fruition (although Perry ended up playing guitar on two of the album's songs).

While the rest period helped recharge a few batteries, it did little to alter the sense of excess that permeated the Aerosmith camp on every level imaginable. "We'd gotten to that dangerous point where we could afford our vices," Tom Hamilton later observed. "We all had our mansions, our Ferraris, and our never-ending stashes."

The situation had gotten so out-of-hand that Tyler found his notorious sex drive outweighed by his chemical interests. "I started getting so screwed up that getting fucked-up seemed more important than getting fucked," the singer admits. "Part of me is still bummed out that I didn't have all of the sex I could have had in the seventies. The irony is that I probably got more than I remember because I was having blackouts. We were more interested in examining the finer blend of cocaine from a shipment of dates that came in on the back of some camel with the stamp of a half-moon on it and the star of Lebanon—which, by the way, was laced with opium. That was much more important to me than some girl with big tits."

By the time Aerosmith's next recording commitment rolled around, the novelty of downtime had worn off and the band members were eager to get back to music. But it would soon become very clear that the group was in something less than peak working condition.

Mindful of Tyler and Perry's shaky condition,

David Krebs decided that it would be healthier for the band to record in a quieter, more secluded atmosphere than bustling, temptation-filled midtown Manhattan. The strategy probably seemed like a sensible one at the time. But the resulting album, which would bear the wickedly inappropriate title of *Draw the Line,* would prove to be the first major letdown in the Aerosmith catalogue, marking the first instance in which the band's personal habits would have a noticeably detrimental effect on the quality of its music.

The band, Jack Douglas, and a ton or so of expensive recording gear were dispatched to the town of Armonk in upstate New York, to record in a converted 300-room convent known as The Cenacle. Perry described the scene to *Creem:* "Sixty acres with a great big house, and the Record Plant installed a studio there for us, literally installed a whole studio. I don't know how much it cost us, but it was outrageous. They had a bar and people to serve and I'd wake up at four or five in the afternoon and say, 'One Black Russian, please.' We had motorcycles and Porsches and we'd go cruising around the contryside terrorizing everybody. We had all our friends up there and we'd go shooting off all these guns at the shooting range, just blasting away. . . . We had a great time up there."

Much of the spring and summer of 1977 were spent waiting for the band's two frequently-incapacitated figureheads to get their acts together. Perry had managed to lose his only copy of a demo cassette containing six musical pieces he'd written for the album, and he couldn't remember any of the tunes. Meanwhile, Tyler, whose tardiness in writing his lyrics was becoming something of an Aerosmith tradition, spent a substantial chunk of his time locked in the convent's tower with a shotgun, taking potshots at the animals that inhabited the grounds. On one occasion, he passed out while leaning on his loaded gun.

As the band continued to while away the days with little releasable music to show for their time, studio bills continued to mount and interband relations grew progressively more strained. With their putative leaders largely incapacitated by their nonmusical pursuits, the still functional (and increasingly frustrated) rhythm section whiled away many an hour jamming in the studio—one example: the impishly progressive instrumental "Krawhitham," which later showed up on *Pandora's Box,* and presents some persuasive evidence of how important Aerosmith's three silent partners were to the band's sound.

"Steven and Joe just weren't around," Whitford explains. "They were locked away in their rooms consuming whatever they were consuming. We were still functioning. We still got up in the morning. So Tom, Joey, and I had a lot of time together."

"Usually those two didn't even come down from upstairs," Hamilton recalled. "So we'd drive our Ferraris around Armonk for a while, then jam and record. We had a good time, but then again we didn't."

"From the inside I didn't think anything was wrong," Perry recalls. "But from the outside you could see everything. The focus [was] completely gone. If I kept a journal, I couldn't do a better job of showing exactly where we went south. Especially because I was too fucked-up to actually keep a diary. The Beatles made their White Album; we made our Blackout Album."

In late summer of 1977, despite the band's precariously shaky state and in brazen disregard of the previous year's European misadventure, the challenge of conquering foreign markets proved too much to resist, and Aerosmith launched its second assault on the Continent. The tour was based around a string of festival gigs that management hoped would be less costly and more productive than the prior trip. What the band got was a series of mud-soaked, musically lackluster performances marked by mostly negative press notices, the band members' questionable personal behavior, and the heavy-handed tactics of the band's ever-protective road crew. The trip would be Aerosmith's last European jaunt for more than a decade.

Despite the group's internal problems and its mostly unsuccessful efforts to jump-start its overseas popularity, Aerosmith remained an A-level attraction at home. That fact was handily demonstrated when *Draw the Line* was released just before Christmas of 1977 and went platinum faster than any Aerosmith LP to date. Unfortunately, the music largely failed to justify the fans' enthusiasm, with occasional moments of brilliance scattered across a largely unfocused sonic canvas.

The collection opened credibly enough with the potent one-two crunch of the Tyler-Perry numbers "Draw the Line" and "I Wanna Know Why," but quickly dissipated with the watered-down strut of "Critical Mass," the distended blues of "Get It Up" and the unimpressive Perry-written-and-sung "Bright Light Fright."

Side two followed a similar pattern, starting promisingly with the multilayered crypto-political epic "Kings and Queens," featuring Tyler on piano and Douglas on mandolin, before fizzling out with the distinctly half-assed "Sight for Sore Eyes" (for which Douglas and David Johansen shared writing credits with Tyler and Perry) and the similarly secondhand "The Hand That Feeds." In contrast, the band's straightforward take on the much-recorded nineteen-thirties blues standard "Milk Cow Blues" (another regular feature of the Jam Band's bar sets) seemed a paragon of energy and integrity.

If the music on *Draw the Line* was largely disappointing, at least the album's cover art—a humorous caricature of the band by legendary artist Al Hirschfeld—held some offbeat appeal. The album package also introduced a new, streamlined reworking of the winged Aerosmith logo, snazzily redesigned by former band member Ray Tabano, who by now was firmly installed in the Aerosmith organization's marketing division.

"I don't think *Draw the Line* is as good as *Rocks*," Perry admitted in *Trouser Press*. "It's not as hard-edged. We got a little bit too into it—it was a real self-indulgent album. I like most of the songs on it, but we took our time doing it too much."

"I have demos from the *Draw the Line* sessions that I still listen to in my car," Brad Whitford said later. "There are some incredible tracks that never got on the record."

In reviewing *Draw the Line,* the critics tended to agree that the extra time spent on the album didn't show in the final product. Writing in *Crawdaddy,* Toby Goldstein commented, "The band shows a deadly wear and tear on their creativity which doesn't abate until the album's closing minutes. Solid passages leading inevitably to neat repeat lines are abandoned in favor of repeat lines alone, to the extent that even Tyler does more rhythm accompaniment than lead-singing. Without necessary vocal continuity, songs like 'Get It Up' or 'The Hand That Feeds' never become more than bombastic chants."

Further, Goldstein noted the squandered musical potential evident in the album's grooves. "What is frustrating about *Draw the Line* is that many of its decidedly unoriginal numbers contain deft, captivating fragments." And she wasn't alone in finding the band's arrangement of "Milk Cow Blues" the album's best-realized track. "From the first repeated guitar note, its clarity and crispness form a sharp contrast to the rest of the album," she noted.

Though fans, critics, and the band itself agreed that *Draw the Line* wasn't up to the standards set by its predecessors, Aerosmith remained one of rock's most in-demand live acts. On March 18, 1978, the band headlined the decade's biggest rock festival, California Jam II, sharing the bill with Ted Nugent, Santana, Heart, Dave Mason, and Mahogany Rush, in front of a crowd estimated at 350,000. But the cracks showed in Aerosmith's lackluster set, particularly in Tyler's hazy performance. A journalist who interviewed Tyler before the concert found the singer, who later claimed to barely remember the show, snorting piles of cocaine off a photo of his own face in a Japanese rock magazine.

In a late-eighties *Spin* magazine story on the band, longtime friend Mark Parenteau, a DJ for Boston's influential album-rock station WBCN, remembered Tyler and Perry's sorry state. "Steven and Joe were into wretched excess in every area," said Parenteau. "Every alcohol, every Percoset, every designer drug they could get their hands on.

"I think it was the reality of *being* Aerosmith when they were very young," Parenteau opined. "Steven considered being really high what a rock star *should* be. They lost reality. They had thousands of dollars in their hand every day to go out and spoil themselves, but the big money was never put away. They just forgot to go to work again. They were so high and so rich and so successful that they just became lost."

In the same *Spin* story, a former Leber-Krebs employee recalled the irregularity of cash disbursement on the *Draw the*

Line tour. "All the money came into Contemporary Communications, everyone had Aerosmith Productions credit cards, it was really confusing," the source claimed. "Then someone in the band would ask for three weeks' advances up front. . . . I had to advance money that could have only gone for drugs. The deals were made in my presence once or twice."

10

CRITICAL MASS

Although Aerosmith didn't release a new studio album in 1978, the band remained in the public eye, thanks to a variety of projects that would prove a bit less taxing on the band's increasingly strained creative powers.

First, Aerosmith managed to be virtually the only act to survive producer Robert Stigwood's bloated, Beatle-less film adaptation of the Fab Four's classic *Sgt. Pepper's Lonely Hearts Club Band* album with their credibility intact. In guest-star roles as the nefarious Future Villain Band opposite goody-goody stars Peter Frampton and the Bee Gees, the 'Smithsters were the inappropriately sugary film's token nod to genuine rock 'n' roll bad attitude.

Similarly, Aerosmith's tough, swaggering version of "Come Together" was one of the few tolerable items on the film's desultory (if star-studded) soundtrack album. Both the film and the album were among the summer of 1978's most notable bombs, but "Come Together" emerged as a Top 20 hit.

The band claimed to have taken on the *Sgt. Pepper* project for the opportunity to record with legendary Beatles producer George Martin, who'd been brought aboard as the project's sole link to the Beatles' credibility. Recording "Come Together"—which the band and Martin did in one six-hour session—came easy to this group of fans who'd been covering Beatles tunes since their bar-band days.

"It was really cool to be in the studio with George Martin," Joe Perry recalled later. "You always wondered what it would be like to be in the studio with one of the Beatles, and he was sort of the fifth Beatle. It was kind of intimidating, but we weren't too easily intimidated in those days."

The movie itself wasn't quite as fulfilling. "I haven't been recommending the film to my friends," Perry admitted to *Trouser Press* shortly after its release. "Just because we're in it, it's no affront to me if you don't go see it."

"Doing *Sgt. Pepper's* was hard work—twelve hours a day for three days," Perry told *Creem*. "It gave us some insight into why not to be an actor, but it was all right. Nobody was pulling any star trips, Frampton or the Bee Gees, or anything like that. But, ah, there was a few things they wanted us to do . . ."

One of the band's principal objections involved a scene in the original script in which Tyler's character is killed by Frampton's nice-guy hero Billy Shears. Perry: "We're sittin' there sayin', 'There's no *way* that Steven is gonna get directly offed by Frampton. No way. It's gotta be an accident.' So they switched it and what happens is we're killin' the Bee Gees, and Strawberry Fields pushes Steven off the stage and kills him. So it wasn't Frampton that killed him. [And then] we killed Strawberry, so it was really cool."

Despite the finished film's cringeworthy quality, Perry was perversely proud of Aerosmith's outlaw status in the project. "It's like we're the underdogs in this whole thing," he said. "There you have the Bee Gees smiling with their nice teeth and all that shit, and then you got the close-ups of me and Steven, and Steven's fried and we're both fuckin' . . . out there. My skin is all white because it was winter and we had been in Boston, and there's my face up there in close-up with my fuckin' crooked teeth and my crooked nose. . . . We didn't think the movie was gonna bomb as bad as it did, but I don't think we suffered too badly for it as far as our image goes."

A decade and a half later, in an interview with *Tower Pulse,* Tom Hamilton looked back on the *Sgt. Pepper's* project: "That was an example of how somebody took all the cool experimental stuff from the sixties and seventies and turned it into a lunch box with a picture on it. The fact that we were in it and did something that was kind of nasty and opposite the whole vibe of that movie was a nice symbolic thing. Maybe it was a sign that Aerosmith would survive the whole corporate takeover of rock 'n' roll."

Aerosmith was also represented on the record racks in the summer of 1978 by the multi-artist *California Jam II* double album, recorded at Ontario Speedway during the titular festival. That album included the band's live renditions of "Same Old Song and Dance," "Draw the Line," and "Chip Away the Stone," the latter a memorable tune by band friend Richie Supa, which had become a regular feature of Aerosmith's live set.

The same summer, the band attempted to mount a back-to-the-roots tour of club and small theater venues, apparently to prove to their fans—and, perhaps more importantly, themselves—that they hadn't completely lost touch with their roots and their fans. But the idea of playing smaller venues quickly fell apart amidst mounting interband hostilities. The proposed tour ended up being just two dates, at L.A.'s Starwood Club and Boston's Paradise, billed as Dr. J. Jones and the Interns.

"It was more fun playing that gig than I think I've had in two years," Perry said of the Starwood gig in a *Creem* interview. "There's lots of things you can do in one of the big places—you can use a lot more equipment, you're a lot freer to use the guitars in different ways, and you have a lot more stage to fill—but I think for really getting down, clubs are the best 'cause you see the people. You get an immediate reaction if you fuck up or if you do something good. I couldn't believe how exciting it was. . . . The place was wall-to-wall, and we just opened it up."

Perry also reveled in the fact that, unlike so many supposedly low-key superstar club gigs, the Starwood show was performed for an audience of fans rather than industry insiders. "The day before the gig, our manger didn't even know we were gonna play there," he reported. "We booked the gig ourselves, hired the equipment, everything. So when we tell him, he says, 'Now let's see . . . what can we do with this? You wanna broadcast this live?' And we said, 'We're just gonna play there and that's it.' . . . Our crew told us that Rod Stewart couldn't get in because they said it was too full."

As it turned out, Aerosmith's 1978 summer tour was in stadiums rather than clubs, allowing them to reach more fans while spending less time on the road. To the band's credit, even when playing in the most mammoth venues imaginable, they frequently showed genuine affection and consideration for their audience, as demonstrated by the instance in which the band sent an attorney to a Fort Wayne, Indiana, jail to bail out fifty fans who'd been busted for pot at that night's concert. Also, this time around the group had the stadium venues outfitted with extra speakers and large projection screens to make things a bit more bearable for the inhabitants of Nosebleed City.

Still, the band—who by this point could rarely be bothered to play sound checks—had rapidly developed a rep as a decidedly unpredictable live act, as discovered by those who saw the band headline the Texas World Music Festival, a.k.a. the Texas Jam, at Dallas's Cotton Bowl on the Fourth of July. Sharing the bill with Leber-Krebs stablemates Ted Nugent and Mahogany Rush, along with Heart, Journey, the Atlanta Rhythm Section, Van Halen, Eddie Money, and Head East, Aerosmith gave a decidedly substandard performance (which, oddly enough, was eventually allowed out as a home video entitled *Live Texxas Jam '78*, several years after the fact), with a black-clad Tyler stumbling obliviously through a lackluster set climaxed by a guest appearance from Ted Nugent.

The *Draw the Line* tour continued through the second half of 1978 and early 1979 in similarly halfhearted style, with the band augmented onstage by keyboardist Mark Radice, whose father Gene had produced Chain Reaction's first single as well as the Left Banke's "Dark Is the Bark," on which Tyler had provided backing vocals. On a regular basis, Tyler had to be rousted out of a drugged stupor prior to shows, often needing to be carried to the stage by a crew member. He'd usually click into performing mode once he reached the stage, and generally manage to make it through the show. On several occasions, though, the singer collapsed mid-set, with the rest of the band scrambling to cover for his incapacity. And then there was the time when, at a concert at California's Anaheim Stadium, Tyler stopped the band four songs into the set to sit at the foot of the stage and deliver a rambling monologue to the crowd as his bandmates stood by helplessly.

By now, the Aerosmith touring entourage had swollen to a huge, unwieldy machine whose main function seemed to be to shield the pampered band members from the inconvenient demands of the outside world. The band owned its own Lear jet, so instead of traveling from city to city, the tour party would base itself in a hotel in a centrally located city, traveling back and forth between hotel and venue. This approach had become something of a necessity, due to Tyler and Perry's distinctly unroadworthy physical condition, and the increasing challenge of getting the band members (and their wives and girlfriends) out of their hotel beds every morning.

Small wonder that, even in a decade in which the music world was dominated by excess on every conceivable level, Aerosmith had earned a dubious renown as the most over-the-top band in the business, taking rock-star extravagance to absurd extremes. Writing in the English music weekly *Sounds,* journalist Geoff Barton called Aerosmith "the worst example of the superstar syndrome I've ever come across," recalling a show at Toronto's CNE Stadium, at which he watched the band members board a pair of limos to travel the hundred yards between the dressing rooms and the stage entrance.

Meanwhile, Tyler and Perry's drug-fueled ego battles were flaring to the point of absurdity. Things had gotten so bad that the pair, who by then refused to even sit together in the same limo, would frequently tangle onstage in mid-set, doing their best to undermine each other's performances. On one such occasion, Perry punctured Tyler's lower lip with the end of a guitar string, and the singer retaliated by spitting blood at the guitarist.

"We'd stopped leading our band; we'd stopped giving a shit," Perry later admitted. "We'd go out to play and we'd struggle to get through 'Back in the Saddle,' as opposed to getting out there and moving things ahead. And all of a sudden there were all these new bands like Van Halen taking up the slack. We were just laying down sleeping and other people came in. We just *blew* it."

The band's internal tensions were intensified by the hostilities between various band members' spouses, particularly in the ongoing feud between Tyler's new wife Cyrinda Fox and the famously touchy Elissa Perry. The wives' personality clashes would often spill over into the band members' working relationships, putting an additional edge on the already tangled daily psychodrama that Life With Aerosmith had become.

The band's road crew certainly had its hands full dealing with Tyler and Perry's bad habits, which had escalated to such severe levels that the pair—who'd earned the nickname "the Toxic Twins," through their reputation for ingesting any illicit substance put in front of them regardless of quality or quantity—often seemed to be in competition to see who could rack up the most near-death experiences.

On one occasion, Perry suffered a drug-induced convulsion just as the band's private plane was cleared for takeoff; the flight had to be aborted. On another, Perry shot codeine and woke up hours later in a doorway with the needle still in his arm. Tyler, meanwhile, once lost consciousness while driving his Jeep through the woods, causing his foot to hit the gas pedal and sending the vehicle crashing into a tree. And then there was the time that Tyler broke his ankle stumbling offstage during a show, but was so doped-up that he immediately stood up without feeling any pain.

Despite the tensions brewing in the band's ranks, Aerosmith remained one of young America's favorite rock acts, as demonstrated by the instant success of the double LP *Live Bootleg,* which was released in November and quickly earned the group its sixth platinum award.

Depending on one's point of view, *Live Bootleg's* spartan packaging and raw, semipro sound quality were either a powerful testament to the enduring strength of Aerosmith's garage roots, a brazen slap in the face of the group's fans, or a pointed nose-thumbing gesture toward the makers of the low-fi Aerosmith bootlegs that had proliferated for years on the underground market. However you slice it, the album's purposely ragged approach said a lot about the band's growing restlessness, offering a welcome contrast to the suspiciously slick sound of seventies in-concert discs like Peter Frampton's 1976 *Frampton Comes Alive,* which set the standard for blockbuster double live albums.

Live Bootleg was drawn from a variety of shows from the previous two years along with covers of "I Ain't Got You" (a blues tune earlier popularized by the Yardbirds) and James Brown's "Mother Popcorn," from an April 1973 live radio broadcast from Boston's Paul's Mall. Despite the frequently dodgy sound quality, *Live Bootleg* was an enjoyably gritty document of the ragged-but-right intensity of Aerosmith on a good night, with such highlights as the first appearance of "Chip Away the Stone" (in a different version than the one on *California Jam II*) on an Aerosmith album and a nice rehearsal version of "Come Together"—along with energetic runs through such

Aerosmith standards as "Back in the Saddle," "Sweet Emotion," "Toys in the Attic," "Walk This Way," and "Dream On."

In a *Creem* interview, Perry explained *Live Bootleg*'s purposely ragged approach. "As far as I'm concerned, I didn't want to do a live album because there's so many perfect [live] albums coming out, all doctored and fixed—big deal. . . . I felt like we had to top that, do a real live album, like *Live At Leeds, Get Yer Ya-Ya's Out,* that old Kinks album, or *Got Live If You Want It.* . . . Then we started finding all these old tapes, like the one from Paul's Mall in Boston. It was right after we'd recorded the first album. All we had of it was a two-track tape off a radio broadcast. Everybody said, 'Two-track! We can't put that on an album. Too much hiss, too much this and that. . . .' And we said, 'What the fuck do you think they did ten years ago?'"

In keeping with the warts-and-all concept, *Live Bootleg,* unlike most seventies live albums, was made with minimal studio tinkering. "Anybody who tells you they didn't fix anything on a live album is strictly inaccurate," Perry told *Creem.* "The fixing *we* did was just places where the guitar or the mike went out. . . . I've let stuff go by on this album, like guitar mistakes, and I just don't want to change it. I don't want anybody fixin' it. That was *that* night. There's no multitrack vocals on this to make it sound sweeter or anything like that. In a few places Steven was singing really off, so off that it would be totally offensive to hear, so we took that part of the vocal out, if we could, and put a new one in. But I think there's only one or two places where we did something like that. . . . I'd say we did a total of ten minutes of fixing for everybody on the album."

Whatever its musical merits, *Live Bootleg* certainly served its purpose in temporarily forestalling the necessity of recording a new studio album. Particularly in light of *Draw the Line*'s painfully protracted birth cycle, many in the Aerosmith organization questioned whether the band could overcome Tyler and Perry's interpersonal tensions— not to mention their drug problems—long enough to finish an album's worth of new material.

It was clear to anyone paying attention that Aerosmith was inexorably headed toward some sort of showdown.

11

PUSH COMES TO SHOVE

A December 1978 story in *Circus* had found Perry sounding wasted and miserable backstage after a show at New Jersey's Giants Stadium. "This blows, this really sucks," Perry grumbled. "One hour you're onstage, you're happy . . . then as soon as you walk off, you fucking start hating it all over again, until the next town and the next show. Man, I hate this shit."

Aerosmith still bore the mental scars of an October 1977 incident at Philadelphia's 20,000-seat Spectrum, in which an M-80 thrown by an audience member exploded onstage, injuring Perry and nearly blinding Tyler. Just thirteen months later, five songs into a November 25 concert at the Spectrum, bad luck struck again when an audience member tossed a glass bottle at the stage.

The bottle narrowly missed Tyler, shattering against a PA

monitor and spraying shards of glass in the singer's face, opening cuts on his chin and under his eye, at which point the band retreated from the stage. Offstage, with Tyler pressing a towel to his swollen, bleeding face, the band voted four to one to end the show, and within minutes Aerosmith was off in its limo. "The Philly show was really important to them," a band spokesman later commented. "It was one of the few shows they did a sound check for."

The Philadelphia incidents seemed symptomatic of an increase in the level of violence at Aerosmith concerts, and at rock shows in general. At the aforementioned Giants Stadium show, as the band performed in front of a 50,000-strong crowd, a roll of toilet paper flew out of the audience toward Tyler's head, at which point the singer instinctively retreated to the rear of the stage. "They're not really throwing it at *you*," Tyler said afterwards. "They just want to see what happens, how a rock star reacts—if you're a regular human."

If anyone seemed convinced of his own status as a regular human, it was Joe Perry, who remained decidedly skeptical about his own success. "The more things you do, the more you realize there's no point at which you've made it," he said. "There's always something that you reach for, but there's no point at which you feel you've made it. Like on our '76 tour, I jammed with Jeff Beck. So I've made it? No. I'm glad to find out there's no place you can't get past. The *Sgt. Pepper's* movie showed us more places to go, more things to do. And we gotta keep the kids happy as well. So we can sell three million *Rocks* records . . . but now we better come up with something else."

The eternally self-effacing Perry showed a refreshing lack of ego in his reluctance to play up to his guitar-hero persona. "I don't think about that too much," he told *Trouser Press*. "I know how good I am and how bad I am. I have no illusions about my playing. I did an interview once where the last question was, 'What do you tell somebody who wants to be a good guitar player?' I said, 'I don't know—ask a good guitar player.'"

Speaking with *Creem* in December 1978, Perry revealed his plans for an extracurricular recording project that would give him the chance to spread his musical wings a bit. "I've been wanting to do one for the last few years now," he said. "Last year I couldn't do it because *Draw the Line* was taking a long time. I don't want to do anything that will take away from [Aerosmith]. None of us would. I'll probably even do a couple of Aerosmith songs, just do them differently like I first thought of them when I wrote them. But there's not gonna be any solo career, nothing like that."

Tom Hamilton, meanwhile, went on the record to predict that the post–*Draw the Line* Aerosmith was not in the midst of a sharp decline, as the rest of the world seemed to assume, but on the verge of a musical rebirth. "I think we're going through a renaissance," said Hamilton. "Everybody's really inspired right now. After *Toys in the Attic* and *Rocks,* we were really riding a big wave. We were selling a lot of albums, and we spent a lot of time doing *Draw the Line,* [and] kind of indulged ourselves a little. We went off the road for a while and we stagnated just a little. . . . This year we changed our game a little bit, doing the *Sgt. Pepper's* movie, California Jam, Texxas Jam, some of those real big outdoor shows. . . . At the end of the tour, everybody was wasted, but we were also really high, really sharp. Everybody was stimulated."

As it happened, Hamilton was dead wrong, as would be made clear long before Aerosmith finished the album that would bear the title *Night in the Ruts.* After preproduction work at the band's Boston rehearsal studio, the Wherehouse, Aerosmith moved to Manhattan's Mediasound Studios to record with Englishman Gary Lyons, the band's longtime studio handler Jack Douglas having been fired early in the production process. Lyons, who did double duty as producer and engineer, came to the band bearing a résumé that included work with the hard-rocking likes of Foreigner and Humble Pie.

Almost from the beginning, the *Night in the Ruts* sessions were dominated by the uneasy feeling that things could fall apart at any minute and that the project was more of a salvage job than anything else. Relations between Tyler and Perry had grown so strained that the two would not work in the studio at the same time. Perry laid down most of his guitar parts early in the recording process, but Tyler was such a mess that getting him to write and sing his lyrics was a tortuously slow, frustrating process that ended up wasting considerable time and money.

So much money, in fact, that Leber-Krebs decided to send the band back out on the road to try and make back some of the what had been squandered on the sessions. At a pre-tour business meeting, Perry was presented with an $80,000 room-service bill and informed that he was in debt to the band to the tune of $100,000. Perry was also told that he could rectify the situation by recording a solo album and using his advance to wipe out the debt.

Perry agreed to the solo-album scenario. Not surprisingly, the substance-sodden Tyler (who by his own admission was "totally F.U.B.A.R.—fucked up beyond all recognition"—took great offense at Perry's act of independence, further fueling the substantial tensions between the two. And, since by this point Tyler

Tyler always appreciated his fans. (*Michael Putland/Retna*)

and Perry were barely speaking, the singer never confronted the guitarist directly, stewing over the perceived slight and letting the bad vibes simmer as the band hit the road.

It didn't take long for the tensions to boil over. The inevitable occurred backstage at a hastily convened band meeting immediately after a typically half-hearted show in Cleveland. The hostilities erupted into a nasty free-for-all, with the band members' wives eventually entering the fray. At some point, Elissa Perry poured a glass of milk on Terry Hamilton. That was enough for Joe Perry to decide that it was time to split. "Yes, it's true," Tyler confirms. "We actually broke up over spilled milk."

Perry wasted little time in turning the casual aggregation of musicians he'd been jamming with during *Night in the Ruts'* production delays into a full-fledged band. Armed with a passel of musical ideas—many of them originally earmarked for Aerosmith—Perry enlisted Jack Douglas as coproducer and swiftly recorded the first Joe Perry Project album, *Let the Music Do the Talking*. While the rest of Aerosmith slogged through the remainder of the *Night in the Ruts* sessions, Perry called Hamilton to deliver his official resignation.

"I washed my hands of it," a disgusted Perry recounted in *Creem*. "After a certain point, I said 'No, I'm not going back to New York and just sit around and not do anything.' I said, 'It's *your* album, do what you want with it. You've got my work, you can use it or erase it. I'm working on something else.'"

Meanwhile, the Perry-less Aerosmith, under Tyler's decidedly unsteady hand, limped toward *Night in the Ruts'* completion, with Richie Supa, band guitar-tech Neil Thompson, and Perry's eventual replacement Jimmy Crespo coming in to patch up the guitar tracks. At one point, former Scorpions/UFO guitarist Michael Schenker was suggested by Krebs as a possible replacement for Perry, and was called in to add some guitar, but the eccentric German axeman stormed out of the studio when an understandably punchy Gary Lyons cracked some ill-timed Nazi jokes. Despite it all, Lyons managed to marshal his troops to complete the album just as the latest block of studio time was running out.

When *Night in the Ruts* finally hit the racks in November of 1979, the album, while hardly a classic, was surprisingly impressive in light of the confused period that spawned it. Even the departed Perry (who was credited as a full band member and pictured in the punning cover photos of the group in full coal-miner regalia) agreed that "there was still a lot of good music in those years. There just wasn't a band together enough to back it up."

Indeed, *Night in the Ruts'* musical quality largely belied the confusion of its birth cycle, with numerous touches of humor and humanity peeking through the haze. The opening track, "No Surprize," was a tongue-in-cheek bit of band autobiography that was particularly trenchant in light of Aerosmith's current trials, while "Mia," Tyler's gentle tribute to his new baby daughter, managed to be poignant without being sappy.

The slyly rocking "Cheese Cake" demonstrated that, whatever the band's internal troubles, the 'Smiths were still capable of getting it together when the spirit moved them. "That song was done in one take with no overdubs," Perry remembered. "When I played that track I went from a regular six-string to a lap steel and back, live in the studio. Even though the band was falling apart in every other way, it was a testament to how we were playing."

Equally impressive, at least in light of the fact that their coauthors were barely communicating when they were written, are such snappy Tyler-Perry collaborations as "Chiquita," "Three Mile Smile," and "Bone to Bone (Coney Island White Fish Boy)." Tyler helpfully explained the latter track's subtitle: "A Coney Island White Fish is a scumbag. When you lived by the Hudson River like I did, you always saw these things floating by on their way to sea. They were rubbers—guys would tie 'em up and they'd just keep floating."

Despite the reasonable quality of the album's originals, the general lack of songwriting inspiration was suggested by the fact that no less than three of *Night in the Ruts'* nine songs were covers. Most prominent (and seemingly unlikely) of these was a surprisingly effective reading of the Shangri-Las' torchy girl-group classic "Remember (Walking in the Sand)," which was also released as the album's first single. With original Shangri-Las member Mary Weiss on backing vocals, the track nicely underlined Tyler's roots in sixties New York pop, and his unironically impassioned vocal performance demonstrated that he was still capable of delivering the emotional goods when the mood struck him.

Also present was a competent if unspectacular version of the 1945 blues tune "Reefer Head Woman" (originally credited to "Unknown," with the credit later amended to acknowledge the song's writers, Lester Melrose, Joe Bennett, and Willie Gillum). Rounding out the album was yet another Yardbirds cover, a rather redundant reading of the Keith Relf/Jim McCarty/Jimmy Page composition "Think About It," which the Yardbirds had recorded, appropriately enough, in their waning days of 1968.

It wasn't long before it was time to choose a new lead guitarist for the three-month U.S. tour that management had already booked for the band. Early candidates included the aforementioned Schenker, who had refused to audition following Lyons' unsuccessful stab at levity, and Derringer sideman Danny Johnson. In the end, though, the unenviable job of filling Joe Perry's shoes—not to mention the equally unappealing task of attempting to breathe new life into a band that much of the rock world regarded as a fast-sinking ship—fell to a virtual unknown, Jimmy Crespo.

Like his new bandmates, the twenty-four-year-old, Brooklyn-born Crespo had grown up worshipping the Beatles, Stones, and Yardbirds before turning to harder-edged styles. He'd earned his stripes as a member of a popular NYC club band called Anaconda, and later recorded two unsuccessful albums for RCA with the band Flame, a female-fronted hard-rock combo managed and produced by Jimmy Iovine.

To his credit, Crespo, who officially joined Aerosmith in October 1979, managed to learn the entire stage set *and* add some final guitar touches to *Night in the Ruts,* in the two weeks before the band was set to hit the road. As it turned out, though, Crespo's diligence was largely in vain. After a secret warm-up gig with Steve Marriott's reconstituted Humble Pie at the New York club Privates and a few East Coast concerts, Tyler collapsed onstage during a show in New England, and the remainder of the planned tour was cancelled.

Perhaps it was just as well. The few dates that the band played earned mostly indifferent notices. Reviewing a January 17 show at Buffalo Memorial Auditorium, a local rock paper noted that Crespo lacked "any sort of distinctive style, and showed a remarkable ability for breaking strings at crucial points."

Meanwhile, Joe Perry was forthright about the flaws he heard in *Night in the Ruts,* which became the first Aerosmith album not to go platinum. "I'm not happy with the way the album sounds, 'cause I wasn't there for the mix," he told *Trouser Press*. "I don't claim any responsibility for the sound. But I know the basic tracks; I know the potential was there. . . . When my album comes out I think there's gonna be a big difference in the technique, 'cause I was just starting some new things on the Aerosmith album and for some reason it's not mixed up quite as loud. At least they didn't take 'em off! . . . I expected them to erase all my playing."

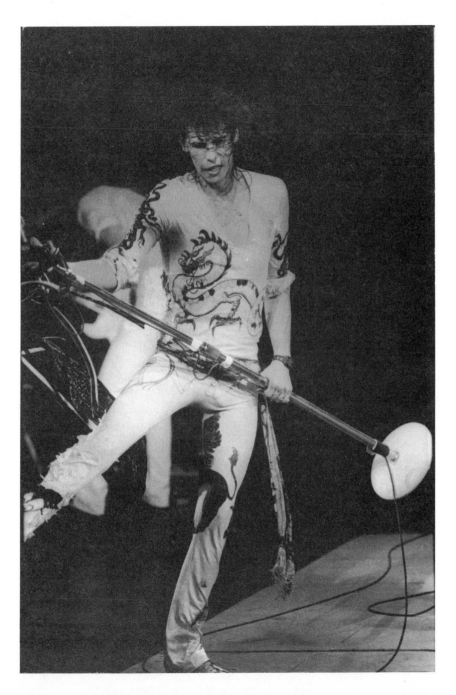

Steven Tyler, before . . . (*Michael Putland/Retna*)

And, uh, after. (*Michael Putland/Retna*)

12

SIGHT FOR SORE EYES

After his official exit from Aerosmith, Joe Perry—who initially maintained his business ties with Leber-Krebs and Columbia, and continued using Aerosmith's Wherehouse as his new band's base of operations—wasted little time in getting his solo career on line, turning the side-project band he'd been working with prior to quitting Aerosmith into a full-time proposition.

Fronting the Joe Perry Project was Ralph Morman, a diminutive, scrappy vocalist whose raw-and-ready vocals recalled Steve Marriott's sandpaper rasp. Morman was an old acquaintance of Perry's who'd been a member of a Boston band called Daddy Warbux, before quitting the music biz and relocating to Florida. Morman was working in a construction job in Florida—but itching to get back into music—when he ran into Perry at a Miami Aerosmith show during the summer of 1979.

Asking the axeman if he knew anyone who needed a singer, Perry responded, "Yeah, me."

The JPP's bassist, David Hull, was a bar-band vet and longtime Perry acquaintance who'd been in the Dirty Angels, a Connecticut combo that had released a pair of albums and toured with Aerosmith the previous summer. Rounding out the Project was an unknown local drummer, Ronnie Stewart, who'd been working in the drum department of the local Wurlitzer music store when he was recommended to Perry by several in the Aerosmith camp.

Whatever the chemical indulgences that were occupying Perry's attention during late 1979 and early 1980, they didn't seem to impede his new band's forward motion. Indeed, the swiftness with which he got the JPP rolling offered an interesting contrast to the molasses-slow movement of Aerosmith's affairs, seeming to confirm the guitarist's frustrations with the group.

The Joe Perry Project's first public performance took place on November 16, just five weeks after Perry's official departure from Aerosmith, and the new band's first album was out by the following March. The Project's first gig was a low-key affair at Boston College's small Rathskellar club, before an audience of a few hundred kids who'd gotten wind of the show mostly through on-campus posters. Steven Tyler was spotted in the crowd early in the evening, but left long before Perry and company hit the stage; Brad Whitford stuck around for the duration.

Though Morman was the band's nominal lead singer, the Joe Perry Project's raggedly energetic early live sets found Perry taking about a third of the vocals himself. "I'm just here for the beer as far as my singing goes," Perry told *Creem,* "but I feel I have a lot of emotion to let out, even though I may not be in pitch all the time. And I think the kids know what I'm trying to get across. At least they haven't thrown any bottles yet."

Whatever his vocal limitations, Perry dominated the evening through his explosive instrumental work and imposing stage presence. With the mostly Perry-written songs from *Let the Music Do the Talking* augmented by some pointedly chosen covers including the old Elvis Presley hit "Heartbreak Hotel," the Bo Diddley (via New York Dolls) chestnut "Pills," the Bobby Womack/Rolling Stones tune "It's All Over Now," and the Music Machine's sixties snot-punk classic "Talk Talk," plus a selection of Aerosmith numbers including "Same Old Song and Dance" (which generally opened the set), "Get the Lead Out," "Bright Light Fright," and "Walk This Way," the guitarist defended his decision to include so many Aerosmith songs in his sets by opining that the JPP was playing them more excitingly than Aerosmith had in years. As it happened, there were not many who cared to dispute that contention.

Indeed, *Let the Music Do the Talking* bristled with the sort of raw, unpretentious gutter-rat energy that had been increasingly hard to find in Aerosmith's recent work. Reunited with producer Jack Douglas, Perry and company had cut the album's basic tracks in just five days in December 1979, before setting out on a short tour of New England clubs and colleges.

Despite this decidedly un-Aerosmithlike efficiency, Perry claimed that Columbia Records had initially been skeptical about the Project. "Aerosmith had been bringing in their albums late, going way over budget, and they thought they'd get more of the same from me," Perry said. "But I convinced them I was a walking, talking viability and not a fuckin' burned-out prima donna."

Despite the label's trepidations, Perry and company finished the album in six weeks and actually came in under budget. "This album was definitely a spurt of energy that was let loose after being fenced up in Aerosmith," Perry told *Creem*. "I'd preproduced, arranged everything. We went into the studio and played the songs *live*. There was no bullshit. . . . The album's like a soundtrack for the live shows." Comparing the *Let the Music Do the Talking* sessions to his recent recording experiences with Aerosmith, Perry told *Creem*, "Different as night and day. Instead of showing up for a party, everyone was there to *play*. And everyone showed up at the same time."

Rather than use his new autonomy to wallow in axe-hero excess, Perry stocked *Let the Music Do the Talking* with compact, melodically direct songs generally clocking in at about three and a half minutes. "I like songs," said Perry. "I wasn't into doing a record of indulgent instrumentals."

The album also made explicit the R&B/funk influence with which Aerosmith had occasionally flirted, finding Perry—in the unusual role of sole guitarist—laying his trademark slash-and-burn chops across sparser, choppier rhythms on tunes like the anthemic title track, "Rockin' Train," and "Discount Dogs."

"I really dig R&B; all the guys in the band are firmly entrenched in R&B," Perry told *Trouser Press*. "That kind of music has always gotten me off so it's natural I would want to write stuff in that vein. I mean, Sly and the Family Stone is one of my all-time favorite bands. And I've always liked James Brown."

Still, it was inevitable that traces of his former band's style would creep in on occasion; it's not hard to imagine "Shooting Star" on an Aerosmith album, and "Ready on the Firing Line" even featured a piece of a riff that also appeared on the *Night in the Ruts* track "Chiquita." Elsewhere, the instrumental "Break Song" rave-up provided a neat two-minute encapsulation of Perry's arsenal of effects, from feedback to fuzztone, and the fanciful "Shooting Star" lyrically summed up Perry's attitude toward his new career, likening his new venture to a space voyage into the unknown.

Reviews of *Let the Music Do the Talking* were mixed, generally praising the new band's increased energy level but also judging Morman's vocals (not to mention Perry's own) not up to the standards set by Perry's previous partner.

Writing in *Rolling Stone*, David Fricke commented, "The Joe Perry Project delivers all of the rock 'n' roll moxie that Aerosmith couldn't manage on the prophetically titled *Night in the Ruts*," but added, "Any singer might feel intimidated by the locomotive pace and guitar-army sound of this album. Any singer except maybe one. If Steven Tyler were here, *Let the Music Do the Talking* would probably be the finest record Aerosmith never made."

Critical quibbles aside, Perry in 1980 was obviously bursting with enthusiasm, talking animatedly about his musical future. "I think with this band, I can extend into the eighties what I thought I was going to do with Aerosmith, but didn't," he claimed. "I've got this inner drive to keep growing, changing. But I'm not going to put Aerosmith down. I loved Aerosmith. I was part of it. I'm proud of it. I think Aerosmith was the epitome of the American heavy-metal band in the seventies, and paved the way for a lot of bands. There would be no Van Halen if it weren't for Aerosmith. But what happened is that Aerosmith got to a certain point, then it was 'What are we going to do now? Just sit back?' And that's what they felt like doing. This band is more a vehicle for my energy."

Perry seemed ready and willing to forsake the

privileges of his rock-star status and start from scratch, playing smaller club gigs rather than ego-stroking arena extravaganzas. "We've been approached to play guest spots opening for some really big acts on the stadium circuit, but I don't want to do that anymore," he said. "If I was in this for the money, I wouldn't have left Aerosmith."

"It's not a step down for me to play in a small club, to be seen by fewer people," he told *Trouser Press.* "You're not sacred; just because you can fill Boston Garden doesn't mean you can't play anywhere else."

He also insisted that the decision to leave was a musical rather than personal one. "If I had left just because of personal difficulties between me and Steven, I'd have left the band a long, long time ago."

Indeed, Perry seemed to be reveling in his new, stripped-down, back-to-basics approach, emphasizing personality and honest energy over spectacle. "When the kids see me out there having a good time getting behind the music and they see the band putting out so much, they really pick up on that energy," he said in *Hit Parader.* He also expressed a kinship for the then-current crop of punk and new-wave bands whose emphasis on no-frills rock 'n' roll recalled Aerosmith's early attitude. "They get out there and they don't use any special effects," Perry enthused. "They just get out there and show the energy and that's what we're doing."

"I don't miss those huge arenas 'cause the vibes in those places are cold," Perry insisted. "When you walk out onstage in a club or theater you feel ten times as much warmth and energy. Most of the people who come to see the shows know what's going on. They're not expecting to see Aerosmith—they're behind the band and are Joe Perry fans. . . . And what's really great is that they're responding to the new songs, stuff they've never heard on the radio."

It seemed clear that Perry was making the most of this new burst of energy. "I feel like nothing can stop me," he told *Creem.* "I've gotten back to basic music, basic *rock 'n' roll.* And a club tour is the way I always wanted to do it. Everybody gets their money's worth. I could have gone on a big arena tour, but I'm not looking to play the rock 'n' roll game anymore and get the most exposure in front of the most numbers. Right now, I feel like a local boy playin' rock 'n' roll in a local club with guys who are real hot, eager to play and gettin' off on it."

In his interviews promoting *Let the Music Do the Talking,* Perry generally spoke affectionately of his former Aerosmith colleagues, but was forthright in noting his disappointment in his later experiences with the band. "It was mechanical," he claimed. "All we had to do was walk out there and play 'Sweet Emotion,' 'Walk This Way,' 'Mama Kin' . . . actually, sometimes we didn't even have to *play.* I could thumb my nose, *drool* on myself—and I did a few times—and the crowds would still cheer. If I tried that tonight, they'd fuckin' throw things at me."

Still, Perry credited Tyler for the lessons he'd imparted during their years together. "Basically, what Steven taught me was *order,*" he stated. "What I taught him was unbridled energy. That's what drew us together at the start and that formed the basis for our love/hate relationship throughout our entire career. All I knew how to do was get up there and rock . . . fuckin' *come.* What he knew was songwriting, so I learned a lot about writing songs from him over the years. Now, I can put together a complete showcase for the energy that I have and always have had. I think I have more energy now than when I was eighteen or nineteen, and I know how to channel it better."

Perry explained that he'd initially intended the Joe Perry Project as a part-time diversion from his work with Aerosmith, but that the logistics of the situation proved unmanageable. "I couldn't see why I couldn't do both," he said in *Creem.* "I'd written enough material for the *Ruts* album and I had plenty of ideas left for *my* album. . . . But they were planning a tour right after the release of *Night in the Ruts,* and I realized at that point, they didn't give two shits if I had a solo thing going. It just didn't matter, they were going to tour, and I thought, 'I don't have control anymore. I've got to make a decision.'" He added that once he made the decision to quit the band, "I felt *relieved.* I suddenly had all this fuckin' freedom and I had a course set in my mind of where I was going."

"I've been wanting to do a solo album for a few years," he told *Trouser Press.* "I just never had the time off 'cause I'd be too involved with Aerosmith. This summer I had a lot of time off so I started putting this together. I just got more and more involved. I would have had to put it all aside for two or three months to go on the road with Aerosmith. I was looking at the same gigs in the same halls; it was, like, enough for me. The past three or four years with Aerosmith have been pretty much all the same. We've been doing the same size halls, nothing different. It was time for a change—all around."

Was it a hard decision to make? "Yeah, it was. Aerosmith has been more than just a band to me for a lot of years. It was the only band I ever went into the studio with. We lived together in the same apartment, it was a way of life. But, for me, it had reached its peak. There wasn't much else we could do. I could see by the way tours were being set up, the way the album was set up, and the way the music was going that it was going to be the same for at least a few more years to come. I wouldn't have been able to initiate changes fast enough to satisfy me.

"Aerosmith stopped being exciting for me," Perry stated. "The other guys obviously have different goals, different reasons for staying; they want to stay together. That's their business. But I reached a point where I didn't want to do it anymore. The others sort of knew there was a chance I wouldn't go on the road with them—and essentially that's me leaving the band. The first thing I said was, 'I don't think I'm going to be able to go on the road with you this time out.' That's how it started.

"They didn't know what I was doing. They were really pissed off for a while, I think—all but Brad. Brad understood from the start. He felt a lot of the same frustrations but I guess he's better able to handle it. I'm sure it's just a matter of time until the other guys come around and realize I just had to do what I had to do. I was wasting my time with Aerosmith, getting frustrated and miserable.

"What drove me to do what I did with Aerosmith is the same thing driving me to do this. It's a search for excitement. I'm not trying to fulfill someone else's dream of being a rock 'n' roller; I just know what needs I have inside, and that's to play in front of crowds where you can feel it coming back. A lot of people—namely the guys in Aerosmith—don't really want to do that."

"Not many people get the chance to have a second career," Perry enthused in the pages of *Hit Parader.* "It's definitely a thrill for me, it's just what I wanted. It seems as though everything up to now has been just warming up. Now it's like the real thing, and it's a real ego thing for me to know that I wrote all the music on *Let the Music Do the Talking.* I don't owe that to anybody. I don't owe anything to anybody anymore."

"It's much more work now," Perry concluded. "I have more responsibility—you can count on lower lows but the highs are higher too. . . . When I'm onstage and the whole band is working . . . it's like driving in a fast car with everything working right. It's amazing."

Perry's ecstatic mood wouldn't last for long.

13

NO SURPRIZE

While a seemingly buoyant Joe Perry was reveling in his new musical freedom, Steven Tyler was stewing in a drug-clouded haze of anger and hurt over what he perceived as the guitarist's betrayal of Aerosmith. Nowhere was the spurned singer's hostility and confusion more evident than in the startlingly nasty interview he gave to *Trouser Press*'s Bill Flanagan, who had just spoken to a relatively gracious, subdued Perry.

Flanagan met with Tyler at the Wherehouse, whose outer walls were freshly spray-painted with fan graffiti begging Perry to return to the fold, while the new Aerosmith lineup prepared for a planned three-month *Night in the Ruts* tour. Tyler gave a rambling, bitter interview claiming that new recruit Crespo had "filled Joe's shoes and then some," insisting that Aerosmith was stronger than ever without Perry, and excoriating the defector for all manner of vaguely defined transgressions.

"There are a lot of things he's been saying in the press lately that just aren't true," Tyler said of his departed bandmate. "If he keeps it up, I'm gonna have to wind up telling the truth about the whole thing and it's not gonna be healthy! So we just say it's a mutual breakup. He's a very bitter man."

Tyler disputed Perry's claim that Perry wrote all the music in Tyler-Perry collaborations, and predicted that the next Aerosmith album would prove that the band could do just fine without the departed guitarist's contributions. Tyler also took issue with Perry's suggestion that Aerosmith had grown complacent and unwilling to take chances.

"Take chances with what?" Tyler fumed. "Well, let me tell you one thing first of all. Playing clubs again was my idea. It was not Joe Perry's idea! I figured, 'What the fuck, let's go back to the kids again.' . . . Nobody in their right mind wants to go back and play clubs the rest of their lives after becoming a big band! . . . I also have an obligation to kids. Sometimes I want to quit the goddamned business but then I think about all the kids that want to hear Aerosmith. You've got to play to them all. You'd never play to them all if you played in clubs.

"As for takin' fuckin' chances, that's what Aerosmith is all about. I don't think there's a better fuckin' album on the market right now than *Night in the Ruts* to show where rock 'n' roll's going."

Tyler also reacted strongly to Perry's suggestions that the band mixed down his guitar parts on *Night in the Ruts*. "If he thinks he's mixed down it's his own damn fault for not being there!" Tyler railed. "He was just pissed off. He was upset about something. He wouldn't come down. I tried my damnedest.

That's when our friendship broke up. I kept calling him up and calling and calling. He just didn't want to come down. That's when I got upset. I said, 'He wants to do the Joe Perry Project? Then let him go ahead and do it!'

"I don't think he's particularly mixed down, either," Tyler added. "If he had something to say, it's there."

The diatribe continued, until Tyler declared that he didn't want to discuss Perry any further. So Flanagan suggested that they talk about the band's upcoming tour—which they did, for about thirty seconds, at which point Tyler interrupted himself, saying, "Listen, don't get me wrong. I'm gonna miss Joe. I'm sure a lot of people are gonna miss him. It's just that his attitude towards the end was not what I'd call on the up and up. I mean, the very fact that he said those things to you . . ."

Tyler also predicted that he and Perry would never be able to sit down and have a beer together, let alone collaborate musically. "I think our relationship is totally dead. He's said too many demeaning things. His wife hates my guts—all kinds of dumb shit. That's just the way it is; rumors, who said this and who said that. I've had my fill of that bullshit. That's what breaks bands up.

"You should talk to the rest of the guys," Tyler continued. "Everybody loves Joe Perry's ass, man. We started off in the beginning like that. For him to spread these fuckin' stories because of a split like this—it's just not right."

Tyler then calmed down. "Isn't it horrible? It can't be just, 'He went his way and we went ours.' He's gotta make up for something. I guess that's the only way he knows how to do it. I still wish him the world. I hope to God he makes it with his band."

A decade and a half later, in an interview with California's *BAM,* Tyler opined that Aerosmith's internal problems could have been resolved, had he and Perry been in more rational frames of mind. "We used to tour eight or nine months out of the year, and the rest of the time we were in the studio, always together. After you do this for a while and become real successful, right up in there, you get this thing that's called 'road warp,' where the dumbest things start tickin' you off and you get really upset about it. . . . We were always out on the road or in the studio. It was fuckin' insane. And a lot of time we went out on the road, we had nothing better to do than stay in the hotels and do drugs, which only added to the complications."

Indeed, Tyler's drug dependency had so impacted his lifestyle that, by 1980, the world-famous rock star was spending much of his time living in squalor in Manhattan's seedy Gorham Hotel, conveniently located near the smack dealers on Eighth Avenue. It was those entrepreneurs who were the chief recipients of the $20-a-day cash allowance he received from David Krebs, who was afraid to give him more, lest he be able to afford to overdose. Broke, in poor health, and prone to acts like squeezing toothpaste into the cracks in the wall to keep out the worms and hands he thought were trying to crawl through, Tyler seemed intent on learning new ways to hit the bottom.

Tyler continued this dissolute existence until one night in the summer of 1980. Riding his motorcycle to pick up Mia's nanny, the alcohol-and-cocaine-besotted Tyler crashed. The singer was nearly killed in the accident, which left him with a separated heel. The injury put Tyler in the hospital for the next six months.

Tyler's friends and business associates had hoped that, at the very least, his latest brush with death would awaken him to the error of his ways and help set him on the straight and narrow. No such luck. Instead, he used his extended convalescence as a convenient opportunity to enjoy the massive quantities of morphine that his doctors were administering on a regular basis, and later, to use his injury as a legit excuse to obtain more painkillers.

14

Steven Tyler spent the remainder of 1980 enjoying the unexpected fringe benefits of his convalescence. Despite his physical and mental condition, Tyler remained stubbornly intent on keeping Aerosmith going, regardless of the band's rapidly declining morale.

While he recuperated from his injuries, the rest of the group worked up new material at the Wherehouse, sending tapes to Tyler to keep him apprised of their progress. But the singer's incapacity combined with his band's already uncertain status to further cloud Aerosmith's future. "We were all burned out to some extent, some more than others," Brad Whitford said. "The cookie was crumbling. Everybody in the band was a rock star."

While waiting for Tyler to recover, Whitford had taken a

leave of absence to record *Whitford/St. Holmes,* an LP of sleekly straightforward rock 'n' roll in collaboration with ex–Ted Nugent singer/guitarist Derek St. Holmes, completing the album in a mere two weeks. When Whitford returned to the fold to begin work on a new Aerosmith album, he found things dragging as unproductively as ever. Finding the band's bloated, unproductive creative process particularly irksome after having finished an entire album in a couple of weeks, sometime in the summer of 1981 Whitford decided that he'd had enough and tendered his resignation. Brad celebrated his new status by taking Whitford/St. Holmes on the road, with bassist Dave Hewitt and drummer Steve Pace completing the lineup, but the setup fell apart when Nugent enticed St. Holmes back into his band.

Meanwhile, Whitford's defection did nothing to dim Tyler's determination to forge ahead at all costs. Years later, the singer admitted that his drive overtook his common sense. "I was so stoned when Brad and Joe jumped ship, I didn't even realize that I was abandoned," he told *Tower Pulse.* "I just wanted to keep Aerosmith together—*fuck them!*"

With Whitford's departure further deepening the atmosphere of gloom within the Aerosmith camp, the band was faced with the unpleasant task of finding another new guitarist. Jack Douglas (back in the Aerosmith fold after producing John Lennon's final album *Double Fantasy*) suggested a replacement in the form of Paris-born, New York–raised Rick DuFay.

DuFay had made his first splash in the rock world—albeit a rather minor one—in an audience photo on the cover of Jimi Hendrix's *Band of Gypsys* album and had subsequently progressed to an unsuccessful, Bill Graham–managed solo career that yielded one album, 1980's Douglas-produced *Tender Loving Abuse*. DuFay's natural swagger and rock-star bearing made him seem a natural for the job, even if the last thing Aerosmith needed in 1982 was another hell-raising extrovert.

In another attempt at an "out of harm's way" change of scene, the band was installed in a rented house in Miami, recording with the help of a mobile recording unit set up outside. Working there and at Miami's Criteria Studios, the band—with Crespo emerging as a key musical contributor—laid down the musical fundamentals for most of the songs that would end up on the album. Unfortunately, getting the barely functioning Tyler to come across with his lyrics proved tougher than ever. The effort became so excruciating that Hamilton, Kramer, and Crespo eventually fled Miami for New York, where they briefly kicked around plans to jump ship and launch a new band with singer Marge Raymond, who'd fronted Crespo's pre-Aerosmith combo Flame.

Meanwhile, DuFay and band friend Gary "Brimstone" Buermele were left with Tyler in Florida, where over the next few months they were charged with getting Tyler functional enough to finish writing lyrics for the stalled album project. They moved the singer to the Sonesta Beach Hotel, where it was hoped that a combiation of sand, sun, and surf would have a positive effect on Tyler's health. Unfortunately, Tyler and DuFay spent most of their time there drinking and doing drugs. (DuFay has claimed that his pleas to get proper professional help for Tyler went unheeded by David Krebs.) Eventually, DuFay and Buermele sought the aid of a doctor who'd helped Eric Clapton overcome his heroin addiction; that doctor directed them to a methadone clinic. When the methadone treatments failed to yield results, they found another doctor, who attemped to treat Tyler with daily injections of vitamin B.

Though various attempts to sober Tyler up proved unsuccessful, the band did eventually manage to piece together *Rock in a Hard Place,* with additional recording completed at The Power Station. The album—which Krebs has said ended up costing $1.5 million—proved something of a victory for Jimmy Crespo, who'd stepped into a barely functioning creative situation and helped whip it into something resembling a viable band, writing the music for six of the album's eight originals and helping to provide some desperately needed musical direction.

All things considered, *Rock in a Hard Place*—released in August 1982 and with production jointly credited to Douglas, Tyler, and Tony Bongiovi—was a surprisingly serviceable effort. While it wasn't likely to make anyone forget *Toys in the Attic,* the album's contents hung together surprisingly well in light of its fractured birth cycle.

The ten-song collection started off on a frantic note with the overwhelmingly hot-to-trot "Jailbait," before easing into the self-assured menace of the Richie Supa–penned "Lightning Strikes," on which Brad Whitford had played prior to quitting the band. "Bitch's Brew" struck a similarly eerie mood with a tightly focused melodic drive and a lyric hinting at unsavory hoodoo doings. That led into "Bolivian Ragamuffin," which wailed with a raunchy intensity recalling the band's most lovably outrageous moments. A metallized rendition of the Julie London jazz-pop chestnut "Cry Me a River" brought side one to an end with a touch of torch.

In the offbeat duo of "Prelude to Joanie" and "Joanie's Butterfly"—the former a spookily atmospheric flight of fancy; the latter a multipart mini-opera that ranges from pastoral acoustic textures to hard-headed rock noise—some unexpected instrumental moves combine with some of Tyler's most enticingly impenetrable lyrics. Meanwhile, "Rock in a Hard Place (Cheshire Cat)" found the band revisiting the brass-laden hard-swing approach with impressive results, while the hard-charging "Jig Is Up" simply hit like a ton of bricks. The album concluded on a note of booze-clouded regret with "Push Comes to Shove," a bluesy barroom singalong, with Tyler delivering his best late-night growl. Under the circumstances, Aerosmith had acquitted itself amazingly well, sounding like a band with a future rather than the sinking ship that insiders knew it to be.

With the just-launched MTV still unproven as a promotional vehicle, Aerosmith tackled the unfamiliar music-video medium head-on in support of *Rock in a Hard Place* starting with a conventional clip for "Lightning Strikes," which unconvincingly depicted the pampered rock stars as dangerous street punks. That inauspicious beginning was followed by the questionable brainstorm of filming no less than *three* more videos— "Bolivian Ragamuffin," "Bitch's Brew," and, inexplicably, "Sweet Emotion"—in 3-D. As with virtually every other attempt to shoot in 3-D since the gimmick's debut in the early fififties, the depth process proved impractical for general use, requiring the viewer to wear uncomfortable paper glasses, which didn't work all that well anyway. Following an elaborately staged debut at the chic New York disco Studio 54, the three expensively lensed clips were barely shown to the public.

The temporary high afforded by the near-miraculous achievement of squeezing a respectable album out of the band's sticky sitaution was quickly overshadowed by the more immediate challenge of getting Aerosmith—which hadn't played live in over two and a half years—together enough to get back on the concert trail. After some rehearsals at Privates in New York, the band moved its full production to the 1,200-seat Concorde Theater in New Hampshire, where a full two months was spent rehearsing and partying.

The *Rock in a Hard Place* tour began in the fall of 1982, with the band's performances reportedly varying from incandescent brilliance to shoddy ineptitude. Considering Tyler's fragile condition, the tour went as well as could have been expected. With an eye toward Tyler's frequent onstage shakiness and his inconvenient habit of losing consciousness during shows, the band and its stage crew had devised a system of hand signals to alert each other when the frontman seemed on the verge of collapse. The crew was also responsible for keeping Tyler away from fans prior to shows, lest anyone hand him any substances stronger than the ones he was already ingesting. By this point, tour comanager Rich Guberti was in charge of physically carrying the unconscious Tyler around hotels, airports, and backstage areas; he also had the potentially dangerous job of wresting him out of bed in the morning.

While Tyler had found a prolific new writing partner in Crespo, the relatively clean-living guitarist was less than ideally suited to Tyler's social requirements. As the tour continued, Rick DuFay warmed to his new role as Tyler's chief carousing partner, and many around the band worried that the match was a recipe for trouble. While DuFay rationalized his participation as an effort to keep the singer out of even worse trouble he might get into if left to his own devices, the combination ultimately created more problems as DuFay fell further into abuse. During a band flight to Hawaii, for example, DuFay had to be physically restrained from ejecting himself from the aircraft.

Despite Tyler's continuing unreliability, and the rest of the band's growing resentment of same, Aerosmith still managed a few musical high points during the *Rock in a Hard Place* tour. At two April stadium shows in Miami, grandly dubbed the Super Bowl of Rock, the band—stuck in the humbling position of opening for Journey, a depressing indicator of Aerosmith's slipping popularity—pulled together to deliver a set that witnesses agree blew Journey and bill-mates Bryan Adams and Sammy Hagar off the stage. Even so, Tyler still managed, mid-set, to vomit on Journey manager Herbie Herbert's shoes.

In view of the band's spotty performances and its rapidly sinking prestige, it's not surprising that *Rock in a Hard Place* sold quite poorly by Aerosmith standards, falling even shorter of the platinum mark than *Night in the Ruts* did. Typically, Tyler attributed this to insufficient promotion on Columbia's part rather than subpar music or the band's tarnished reputation. "There was no promotion," he griped to *BAM*. "Kids didn't know it was in the stores. I don't know whether it was because CBS had fired all their good people or what, but we just needed new blood."

All in all, the photo of Stonehenge on the cover of *Rock in a Hard Place* was a bit too close to the then-current film spoof *This Is Spinal Tap* for comfort. "I was real high at the time that movie came out," Tyler remembers. "And Aerosmith was sinking—we were like a boat going down. That movie was way too close, way too real. I freaked. I took *Spinal Tap* real personal."

15

GOING DOWN

Aerosmith's massive stardom had long allowed the band members to isolate themselves from the responsibilities of the adult world. With managers and crew members to execute their every whim, the 'Smiths were allowed to exist in a blissful state of extended adolescence for the first decade of the band's recording career.

But the band's protective armor began to crack in the early eighties, and the musicians eventually found themselves having to deal with everyday reality on their own. Steven Tyler and Joe Perry both proved themselves to be distinctly unsuited to the challenge. While Tyler was struggling to keep Aerosmith afloat and his own head above water, Perry had his own problems to contend with.

The axeman's drug use had left him in no condition to

carry out the responsibilities of band leadership, and his instability was reflected in the band's spotty progress. His consciousness awash in alcohol and various chemicals, Perry was so out of touch that he was unaware of the existence of *Aerosmith's Greatest Hits*—a best-of collection released by Columbia as a commercial stopgap in October 1980, when it became apparent that it was going to be a while before the band would be delivering a new studio album—until he was asked to autograph a fan's copy.

The initial buzz of musical freedom and personal liberation offered by the Joe Perry Project quickly gave way to a series of lineup changes and questionable business decisions, none of which did much to help the Project's commercial prospects. Ralph Morman left the band in the fall of 1980—fired, ironically enough, by the alcoholic Perry for excessive drinking. After being replaced briefly by one Joey Mala, Morman's shoes were filled by singer/rhythm guitarist Charlie Farren in time for the Project's sophomore outing, the June 1981 Columbia release, *I've Got the Rock 'n' Rolls Again.* That disc, recorded with producer Bruce Botnick at the Boston Opera House, presented a somewhat more focused vision of its predecessor's blues/boogie/soul hybrid, but its unspectacular sales led to Columbia terminating Perry's record deal. In 1982, Brad Whitford joined the Project for a monthlong tour, briefly reuniting Aerosmith's classic guitar team; much to the disappointment of Aerofans, Whitford didn't stick around long enough to record with his old partner.

The Joe Perry Project had originally been managed by Leber-Krebs, and subsequently by Boston-area concert promoter Don Law. By 1983, Perry's career was being guided by Tim Collins, another Boston-area promoter, and his partner

The best and the brightest. *(Ross Marino/Retna)*

Up with people. *(Katia Natola/S.I.N.)*

Joe Perry does his thing.
(Fin Costello/ Retna)

Innocence soiled.
*(Jodi Summers
Dorland/Retna)*

America's favorite working dads. *(Katia Natola/S.I.N.)*

The terrible twosome
share an intimate moment.
(Fin Costello/Retna)

Joe Perry, seen here with guitar and hair. *(Liane Hentscher/S.I.N.)*

Toxic no more. *(Fin Costello/Retna)*

Mighty mouth. *(Phil Regendanz/S.I.N.)*

Steve Barrasso, who landed the Project a new deal with MCA. The band's third and final album, and its sole MCA release, was the self-produced *Once a Rocker, Always a Rocker,* which found Perry leading an all-new lineup with singer Mach Bell, bassist Danny Hargrove, and drummer Joe Pet.

Unfortunately, by the time the album was released in September 1983, it was already clear that MCA's new president, controversial former Eagles manager Irving Azoff, did not consider the Joe Perry Project to be amongst the label's top priorities. Not surprisingly, *Once a Rocker* sold a relatively paltry 40,000 copies—roughly one-sixth of what *Let the Music Do the Talking* did.

Though it was unquestionably the weakest of Perry's three extracurricular efforts, *Once a Rocker, Always a Rocker* wasn't without its merits, revealing a hitherto unsuspected penchant for social commentary in the form of "Women in Chains," a cover tune which Perry first heard on a demo by an obscure Nashville bar band, and whose pro-feminist lyrical sentiments were miles away from the leering lyrical stance Aerosmith was known for. Perry's emerging political consciousness also asserted itself in the benefit shows the Project performed for such causes as gun control and Agent Orange victims.

The JPP's second and third efforts, while respectable enough, had failed to expand the audience won by *Let the Music Do the Talking.* Perry, possessing neither the focus nor the energy to salvage his solo career, acknowledged the writing on the wall and called an end to the Project. He then drifted into various low-rent recording projects, producing demos for local bands while pondering his next move.

With his career stalled, Perry's personal life wasn't faring much better. His finances already a mess, the strung-out guitarist—who was often spotted hobbling with a cane around the Allston section of Boston, looking to score dope—lost most of his remaining money to Elissa in a traumatic divorce settlement. Broke and depressed, he ended up sleeping on Tim Collins's couch.

According to his DJ friend Mark Parenteau, the experience of bottoming out ultimately had a humbling effect on the faded superstar. As Parenteau told *Spin,* Perry "found himself on the streets of Boston by himself, and I think that sort of jolted him into reality. . . . It was a low period for Joe, but it was actually strength-giving. Being out on his own got him a lot more clearheaded in the long run."

"I got so depressed there were times I wouldn't answer the phone for days," Perry recalled in the rock magazine *Faces.* "I tried to manage myself, going solo, but I managed to almost kill myself. My finances went down the tubes. My nerves were so shot, I'd physically jump every time the phone rang."

Perry also told *Faces* that he'd kicked his drug habits. He said that he'd made the decision to get clean after suffering a pair of seizures while on tour with the Joe Perry Project. "It was like a fuse snapped," he recalled, "somewhere in North Carolina. I was out seven minutes each time. Once, in the afternoon on the way to a gig—I woke up in an emergency room—and then, onstage in this steaming, packed club. I went down after the third song. I'd had some close calls before, but not two in one day, and I got to thinking a lot about friends of mine who'd died. I was stagnating. I wasn't takin' care of business. I wasn't writing."

His biggest problem, Perry told *Rolling Stone*'s Steve Pond, was "Mostly heroin. Mostly. A lot of people get strung out on one specific drug, but I'd do anything. It was a strange potpourri. But maybe that variety kept me from going completely over the deep end.

"Just to make the record clear," Perry continued, "I went someplace for a while, had my blood changed, and got cleaned out."

A decade later, looking back on his work with the Joe Perry Project, Perry commented to *Tower Pulse,* "The first grouping was the one that had the most fire for me. I was really fueled by anger. Then I felt like I was treading water on the second two [albums]. I dunno, I really had fun doing it when I was doing it, but it really made me realize what I had with Aerosmith."

"I had gotten my rocks off," Perry said to *Creem.* "I had a lot of stuff that I wanted to get off my chest, and I really enjoyed being the boss of my own project. But, as you can probably see by the turnover of members, there was a lot of talent, but the personalities didn't click. And the last Project was more a get-along-with-the-guys than the talent. So that's when I broke the Project up and figured I'd try doing a little journeyman work—write with this one, work with that one, play on this one's album."

Perry's career was in such a rut that he was considering accepting a sideman position in Alice Cooper's band. Fortunately, that move would soon turn out to be unnecessary.

Tyler very often had quite a lot on his mind. (*Steve Granitz/ Retna*)

16

JIG IS UP

Aerosmith's *Rock in a Hard Place* tour dragged on through the remainder of 1983 and the early months of 1984. Considering Tyler's condition, the tour was hardly the failure that it might have been, but it was something less than the raging success that probably would have been necessary to jolt the band out of its all-consuming doldrums. Although the band had pulled off a relatively impressive number of respectable shows, fans and critics—and, despite his vocal protests to the contrary, Tyler—knew that Aerosmith just wasn't the same without Joe Perry and Brad Whitford.

Despite some attempts at laying down some new tunes written by Crespo, DuFay, and Hamilton, morale in the band was at an all-time low, with even the patience of long-suffering stalwarts Hamilton and Kramer wearing increasingly thin. Eventually, even newcomers Crespo and DuFay had to admit that the band had hit an impasse. Even Tyler realized that drastic measures would be required if Aerosmith was to salvage a viable future out of its current situation.

"I missed Joe Perry," Tyler admitted in *BAM* a few years later. "The magic we'd had in the beginning really wasn't there, even though I'd pretend that everything was OK. Eventually I had to really dig deep and do some soul-searching to figure out what the fuck was goin' on."

Meanwhile, Joe Perry had already written half a dozen songs with Alice Cooper, in preparation for his proposed new role as hired gun in Cooper's band. But the axeman still longed for "the kind of swagger Aerosmith has when we're all together, that Steven and I have when we're playing, that push-pull."

The tensions between Perry and his old partner were obviously easing. All of Aerosmith save Hamilton had jammed with the Joe Perry Project at a gig in Salisbury Beach, Massachusetts. On Valentine's Day, 1984, Perry and Whitford showed up onstage at a surprise Aerosmith club show in Boston. Later, Tyler and girlfriend (and future bride) Teresa Barrick, along with Rick DuFay and his wife, attended a Joe Perry Project show at New York's Bottom Line, and DuFay, of all people, suggested that the two estranged partners bury the hatchet.

In the spring of 1984, Tyler and Perry had a long and relatively cordial phone conversation. "That was kind of the first night the wall broke down," Tim Collins later told *RIP* magazine. "It was the first night [Perry] got serious about a reunion."

"I made Aerosmith work and I could work with any musicians and have a real good time, but it really wasn't happening," Tyler said. "So I went and saw Joe a couple of times and talked about it, and he said that, yeah, he felt the same way. It had been about three years since we'd seen each other, and in that time apart a lot of the wounds had healed themselves. So we eventually got the whole band together in a room, and it almost felt like things were levitating, there was such magic."

With word of a reconciliation in the air, Tyler and Hamilton were openly ecstatic over the news, though Kramer was initially resistant, still resenting Perry for having left the band in the lurch. Once Kramer came around, the classic Aerosmith lineup was back in place.

Perry, for one, seemed distinctly relieved. "There was a lot I couldn't express, a lot of screwed up, personal problems, my own personal problems," he told *Faces*. "I had to break away. But now I feel like I have to be back here. Lookin' back, I really think we just needed a time away from each other, that's all."

Meanwhile, in a *Rolling Stone* interview, Tyler claimed he'd always expected the original band to reunite, and opined that it was inevitable that he and Perry would patch up their differences. "I hated his guts," Tyler admitted. "I said, 'I never want to fucking play on the same stage with you again.' But that's road warp. Time heals all wounds. Joe is nothing without me, and I'm nothing without him. It's like David Lee Roth is nothing without . . . what's that guitar player's name? Oh, yeah, Eddie Van Halen."

But the mere fact that all five original 'Smiths were agreeable wasn't enough to clear the way for a successful reunion. A convoluted tangle of legal issues needed to be resolved before the band could move forward. Perry was already in the process of suing Leber-Krebs (ultimately successfully) for neglect of legal commitments, and insisted that Collins and Barrasso take over the band's management.

Collins was given the job of clearing the path for Aerosmith to start fresh.

"We did have an enormous amount of legal stuff to sort out, though," said Perry. "We wanted to start with a clean slate with this project—and there'd been a lot of ragged edges in the business end before."

"After we realized that we wanted a reunion to happen, we decided to wipe everything clean, from management to record label to booking agency," added Tyler. "We'd been through it, and we weren't going to take anybody's word for anything anymore."

But clearing the decks contractually was no simple matter. The convoluted nature of the band's production deal with Leber-Krebs/Contemporary Communications (to whom they still owed more product) presented all sorts of complications. "The band were still signed to Columbia, and no one at Columbia would speak to us," Collins told *Rolling Stone*. "They would only speak to Leber-Krebs, who had a production contract for, like, seven more records."

The reunited quintet's first rehearsals took place at a Howard Johnson's hotel in Boston. "You should have felt the buzz the moment all five of us got together in the same room for the first time again," Tyler told *Faces*. "We all started laughin'— it was like the five years had never passed. We knew we'd made the right move."

Collins felt that it was essential at this point to get the band on the road—both to provide a musical focus for the band's renewed energies and to generate some much-needed income. So, after a few low-key club gigs under phony names, the band launched the 70-date "Back in the Saddle" tour, announcing to the world that the real Aerosmith was back.

With the threat of lawsuits already looming, playing concerts presented the potential of additional claims from Leber-Krebs, which might involve seizure of box-office receipts. So the resourceful Collins, with financial help from the Monterey Peninsula booking agency, cagily concocted a separate corporation for each show, so that the box-office take couldn't be seized by creditors.

While Aerosmith's reputation for on-the-road unreliability initially frightened off some concert promoters, the "Back in the Saddle" trek was a significant success, both financially and musically. "We've still got a lot of Aerosmith in us," said Tyler. "We're putting some changes in the old stuff, and it really steams up. . . . The point of the tour is to hit the places where we know we have solid fans and get our stage chops back. It *has* been a while."

"As we're playin' we're gettin' so fuckin' tight it's like when we were first playin' clubs," Perry added. "It's that solid background that gives you the edge when you hit the big stage."

The 105-minute sets included material from all of the band's albums except *Draw the Line*. Although they played no new songs, the group did tackle "Let the Music Do the Talking" from the first Joe Perry Project album, which seemed tailor-made for Aerosmith, taking on new resonance in light of Tyler and Perry's mended working relationship. "We do it in three-part harmony—Steve, Joe, and myself," said Whitford. "It's the first time we've ever done anything like that. . . . Joe's also doing a version of Hendrix's 'Red House.' Gives Steven a chance to go backstage during the middle of the show to blow dry his hair, shine his shoes, and such."

Though the band had vowed to clean up its act substance-wise, some of its destructive old habits reasserted themselves, most disastrously at a show in Springfield, Illinois, where Tyler had a few drinks before going onstage, and stumbled through a sloppy, virtually incoherent show. At one point, the singer started playing with Hamilton's bass pedals, leading an annoyed Hamilton to whack Tyler with the neck of his bass. When a fan grabbed his scarf, Tyler fell off the stage. The band walked off in disgust and, according to one insider, "stayed pissed at Tyler for about twenty-four hours" before continuing the tour.

"We screwed up," Whitford said of the Springfield show. "I guess we had to keep our image as troublemakers."

As it turned out, the Springfield disaster proved to be something of a catalyst in the band's new quest for sobriety. "The turning point was in Springfield," Collins told *BAM*. "Everyone was depressed. The band had just gotten back together and they were going to break up. But we rallied about three o'clock in the morning at my hotel room in some shitty little Holiday Inn. I realized that this was the moment to rally around the band and confront the enemy. The enemy wasn't Steven. The enemy was the drugs and alcohol."

On balance, though, the "Back in the Saddle" tour proved to be exactly what Aerosmith needed, launching the reunion on just the right note of organized mayhem. "Now everyone knows I don't have throat cancer, and that Joe can still stand up, and that Brad is still alive," Tyler told *Rock* magazine. "That's the reason we did a tour without having put out an album first: to kill all the bullshit rumors that are going around about the band."

Reviewing a show at San Diego's 3,000-seat Golden Hall, the *Los Angeles Times'* Matt Damsker wrote, "By now, Aerosmith performs with the polish and passion of men who've learned their lessons well. Tyler commands as the prancing, Jaggering jester—scarves streaming, his voice shrill yet rebel-soulful—while Perry is the lucid, fast-fingered flash point, sparring with Whitford as Hamilton and Kramer thunder skillfully." Just as importantly, Damsker observed, the audience was as enthusiastic as ever, "rapt and responsive, from start to finish, as Aerosmith delivered its fierce, sardonic anthems. . . . Aerosmith may have trouble withstanding its inner turbulence, but so far its best music is standing the test of time."

"There's nothing like an Aerosmith groove," Tyler raved to *Spin.* "Everybody out there is trying to do something new, which is great. We do that, too, but Aerosmith is still Aerosmith."

Despite the reunion tour's encouraging results, the reconstituted quintet's return to its former heights of success was still by no means insured. During the group's decline and extended absence from record racks, a new generation of young and generally inferior bands—many of whom made no secret of their debts to Aerosmith's style and attitude—had arrived on the scene to steal Aerosmith's thunder. "We paved the road, so to speak," Tyler told *Rolling Stone.* "So why not fucking get in our cars and drive down it again?"

Even in the face of the new competition, Aerosmith seemed as cocky as ever. "We've been on the road long enough to get it down to a fine art," Perry said proudly. "The Quiet Riots and all those guys with the leather and studs and the stacks of Marshall amps that aren't turned on better watch out. We *are* the band your mother warned you about."

As if to prove the point, Perry joined L.A. lite-metalists Ratt onstage at the Centrum in Worcester, Massachusetts, for a rendition of "Walkin' the Dog," which both bands had covered on record. "I'm flattered by a band like Ratt," Perry told *Rock*. "Their guitar player even came to our show in San Diego; they have no compunction about saying that they were influenced by us."

"Ratt and Mötley Crüe copped all my clothes and everything," Tyler commented in *Spin*, "and it's like me saying, 'Well, I'm just going to go out in my dungarees and play.' Fuck that! I started something great, I'm proud of it, I love it, and if they copy me that's all right, but I'm still going to wear it because I wear it better."

Another thing that Aerosmith found had changed in their absence was that the business which they'd helped build in the seventies had risen to new levels of financial excess, and on the road the band found itself pulling in sums of money even more outrageous than the ones they'd made the first time around. Some estimates of Aerosmith's take from the "Back in the Saddle" tour ran as high as three million dollars—the band received an advance of nearly half a million dollars from a firm selling T-shirts on the tour.

"I know everybody's gonna ask if we got back together for the money, and of course we did," Perry joked in *Rolling Stone*. "No, it's fun to have the money come in, but the reason is definitely the pleasure we get from playing together again."

Perry has expressed the opinion that the issues left unresolved by the band's original disintegration may have had something to do with the dramatic nature of its comeback. The guitarist insisted that Aerosmith still had something left to prove. "We hadn't reached our creative pinnacle yet when we were put on hold for a few years," he said. "So when we started over there was a lot of mountain left to climb. It's not like our best album was *Rocks* and since then we've just been doing it for the money."

"As far as I'm concerned, we're back for another ten years," Perry concluded. "As long as we don't kill each other, we'll be fine."

The kings in repose. (*Greg Freeman/S.I.N.*)

17

GET IT UP

After getting out from under its Columbia/Leber-Krebs commitments, Aerosmith was free to reciprocate the interest of Geffen Records A&R head John Kalodner, an eccentric but effective mover and shaker who'd built a reputation for reviving the careers of hard-rock warhorses. Early supporter Clive Davis also had shown interest in signing Aerosmith to his Arista label, but Collins chose to go with Geffen, which had more of a track record with rock acts.

"Aerosmith was one of the great rock bands. And I knew it could be one again," said Tim Collins, who was fully aware that the band had some serious work to do if it was going to revive its past glory. "They had climbed the mountain once. And they had to climb it all over again."

Fortunately, Kalodner's vision of Aerosmith coincided

nicely with that of Tim Collins, and the veteran A&R man would quickly prove to be exactly the sort of supporter and creative advisor that the group would need to recapture its former glory. One of the new team's first decisions was to match the band with a new producer who could move their sound into the eighties without altering the band's fundamental character. George Martin's name was brought up at one point, but the musicians weren't thrilled with the idea of recording at Martin's AIR studios on the Caribbean island of Monserrat. The job eventually fell to Ted Templeman—a well-liked Californian who'd produced Van Halen's first six albums, as well as working extensively with the Doobie Brothers—who'd long expressed interest in working with Aerosmith.

The band was bursting with energy and enthusiasm when it entered Fantasy Studios in Berkeley, California, in July 1985 to record its comeback effort, *Done with Mirrors*—even if the batch of songs Tyler and Perry had hastily tossed together in the month prior to the sessions was something less than stellar. The musicians spent their first two days in the studio running through the new songs with Templeman and engineer Jeff Hendrickson, little suspecting that Templeman was covertly capturing those raw run-throughs on tape, with some of those rough early takes subsequently ending up on the finished album.

Done with Mirrors—whose recording was completed the following month at The Power Station in New York—recaptured some of the rocking rawness and cocky attitude of Aerosmith's best work, but ultimately suffered due to the material's inconsistent quality. Perry would later confess that the band "went in with some riffs and winged it," rather than starting with fully thought-out compositions.

The fact that the album's most exciting feature was a remake of the six-year-old Joe Perry Project tune "Let the Music Do the Talking"—which Perry had originally written for Aerosmith before his departure, and which the band had made its own on the reunion tour—was just one indication that *Done with Mirrors* was something less than the decisive comeback that fans might have hoped for. Yet the honest grit of the band's performances kept the disc from being a complete washout.

Despite *Done with Mirrors'* vague air of disappointment, the album had its moments of quintessential Aerosmith brilliance, most notably in the pummeling "My Fist Your Face," which, in four and a half minutes, blew several years' worth of dust off of the band's reputation. Elsewhere, "Shame On You" boasted a vicious funk hook, while "Gypsy Boots" and "The Hop" rocked with sufficient levels of ferocity, and "She's On Fire" recalled Led Zeppelin's heathen fusion of American blues and Eastern motifs. Yet undistinguished, overly casual tracks like "Shela" and the punningly titled "The Reason A Dog" betrayed a half-finished feel that hinted at the cause of the album's deeper problems.

Oddly, the quite impressive "Darkness," a mid-tempo number of compellingly foreboding irony, was relegated to cassette and CD bonus-track status—a distinction which would become a moot point once vinyl fell out of fashion a couple of years later.

Tyler explained the new album's title to *BAM*. " 'Done with mirrors' is that old expression used to explain success. You know, when a magician saws a lady in half or pulls a rabbit out of a hat, the cynics always sum it up by saying, 'It's all done with mirrors.' Well, a lot of skeptics also followed Aerosmith around, and whenever we did something right, they'd ask us how we did it. Now we tell 'em it's all done with mirrors. We're through explaining ourselves."

On balance, *Done with Mirrors* was a competent and respectable, if scarcely earth-shattering effort, which, even if it didn't fully recapture the spirit of the band's best work, came close enough to bode well for Aerosmith's long-term prospects.

Nevertheless, the album didn't live up to sales expectations, selling a respectable but less-than-spectacular 400,000; particularly disappointing when one considers that all of the band's prior albums (except for the transitional *Night in the Ruts* and *Rock in a Hard Place*) had sold upward of a million apiece.

Done with Mirrors' relative lack of success proved to be a blessing in disguise, however, providing the band with a much-needed reality check. Times had indeed changed, and the mere existence of new Aerosmith product was no longer enough to guarantee an instant smash. *Done with Mirrors'* disappointing reception was something of a career wake-up call, and the band's options boiled down to two choices: redouble their efforts with a new sense of responsibility or give up the ghost altogether.

Tom Hamilton is philosophical about the gradual nature of the band's comeback: "It's an illustration of priorities," he told *Tower Pulse*. "*Done with Mirrors* was done when ours were divided between getting high and having fun—total nonmusical fun. It's a good album. I like it, but it's not what I had in mind as far as that big statement that we're back."

Just how much the music world had changed—and how much Aerosmith hadn't—became clear when the fivesome undertook a string of eight outdoor shows two months prior to

Done with Mirrors' November 1985 release, and during a world tour in support of the album the following January.

The band found that its audiences consisted mainly of longtime fans rather than new, younger converts. The kids, meanwhile, were busy listening to newer, blatantly Aerosmith-influenced outfits like Mötley Crüe, Twisted Sister, and Ratt, who often seemed as interested in their visual stances as they were in their songs, and whose connection to their pre-rock roots was considerably less acute then Aerosmith's.

"The blues are our fuckin' roots," Tyler told *BAM*. "A lot of other bands out there, they dress up like I used to dress, but there's no fuckin' middle to what they play. No soul. There's no main vein runnin' down the middle of it."

Tyler seemed positively giddy to be back at the helm of the band he'd fought tooth and nail to keep alive. "I feel like it's ten years ago again," he beamed. "I feel like the band never was, and here we are starting out at the beginning again."

But some old habits die harder than others, and those of the band members were once again putting Aerosmith's future in jeopardy. The band members' vows to stay sober had quickly fallen to pieces once they hit the road. "The *Done with Mirrors* tour I remember not remembering anything from the night before," said Perry. "I used to drink to blackout, and it wouldn't be any big deal, but it got to be every night. I'd have a few beers while I was warming up and then wake up the next day. I'd have to call somebody to find out how I played."

The final leg of the tour was cancelled, as were projected visits to Europe and Japan, owing to the band's precarious physical condition. Tyler's drinking had inflicted severe damage upon his much-abused liver, while his heroin use remained an endless source of worry. Perry wasn't far behind, indulging in a wide variety of abuses, while Hamilton still suffered from a cocaine problem and Kramer and Whitford were still battling drinking problems.

Eventually, Tim Collins, the man who'd taken on the thankless task of getting rock's most notorious drug band on the straight and narrow, presented the group with an ultimatum—choose drugs or music.

Surly to bed, surly to rise. (*Steve Double/S.I.N.*)

18

MONKEY ON MY BACK

The first salvo of Aerosmith's all-out war for sobriety was fired when both Collins and the band confronted Steven Tyler about his drug use—a bit hypocritical perhaps, considering his bandmates' still-raging habits, but also an indication of the seriousness of Tyler's condition. Even in his addled state, Tyler realized that things had gotten out of hand, and that action needed to be taken.

Tyler spent a month attending a substance-abuse program, where he was warned that his treatment would be for naught if his bandmates continued using. So it was mutually agreed that the entire band—and, for that matter, everyone within the Aerosmith organization—would clean up en masse. Collins checked the entire band into the Pennsylvania-based rehab center known as the Caron Foundation, where the musicians were put through a twelve-step program that proved traumatic yet ultimately effective.

As Tyler put it, "I did drugs for so damn long that I had to go to a place to learn how *not* to do them."

"It was a slow process," Kramer explained to *Musician*. "One guy would get it and he'd work on another, and there would be two, then three, then four, then all five. . . . We knew it could only work again if we were drug- and alcohol-free."

"For years I was thinking, 'Poor Steve, he has to go to rehab. *I* can control it,' and I'd be driving to my dealer," Perry admitted in the same story. "Or I'd say to my manager, 'Steven's terrible. He's got to go away. *I'm* going to the Cayman Islands to have a vacation to get away from my dealer.' That's what *I* was gonna do, 'cause *I* didn't have as bad a problem as Steven."

"Finally Steven and I made a pact," continued Perry. "I'd never been to a rehab, and he'd been to three, I think. And it was like, 'Steve, you go and I'll go.' I waited for the birth of my son, and I went. Everyone else followed along in his own time. But it was really a trip. I didn't know if I would ever have fun again, or if I would like music again. I guess what proved it for me was *Permanent Vacation* and getting out there to play again. It started feeling like the old days."

Tyler and Perry were still using when they recorded their contributions to hip-hop trio Run-DMC's 1986 rap reworking of "Walk This Way." With the help of an amusing promotional video featuring Tyler's best scene-stealing mugging and Perry's finest axe-hero moves, the track (which became a number 4 single in the States and rose to number 8 in Britain) accomplished what *Done with Mirrors* couldn't—making Aerosmith seem relevant and contemporary again in the eyes of the music industry.

The collaboration couldn't have seemed particularly outlandish for Run-DMC, whose DJ Jam Master Jay had scratched beats and breaks from *Toys in the Attic* when Run-DMC first began performing. But it was a brave move for Aerosmith, coming at a time when most white mainstream rock fans—and, for that matter, white mainstream rock *bands*—generally reacted against hip-hop as violently as they had against disco just a few years prior. The historic collaboration proved to be a crucial turning point in the long-overdue fusion of white rock and black rap, and helped restore Aerosmith's old rep as an innovative, forward-looking rock act; it was also a nice gesture in light of Boston's long history of racial tension.

Tyler and Perry were reportedly paid $8,000 by Run-DMC's management, Rush Productions, for the five-hour session, during which *Spin* writer Sue Cummings observed Tyler and Teresa Barrick disappearing into a nearby bathroom with a jeweled cigarette case and emerging "noticeably refreshed."

The new "Walk This Way" was the brainchild of rock-rap wunderkind Rick Rubin, a longtime Aerosmith fan roughly half the age of Tyler and Perry, who'd stated that he "wouldn't mind producing their next album."

"At one point we were talking to Rick Rubin about doing *Permanent Vacation,*" Perry confirmed to *Musician.* "Steven and I were crazed at that point. We figured we'd go into the studio with him and record a song one night. I had methadone in one pocket, some blow in one pocket, some pills in another pocket, and a bottle of rum. So I was set to record. It was so fucked. The next day we listened to the tape and I was just embarrassed about how we must have acted. And the song sucked. It was time for a major change. For me, and for everyone else in the band."

Still, Perry admitted that his days of abuse

hadn't all been dark. "A lot of the time, I had fun," he stated. "No doubt about it. Now I'm stuck in today, [so] it's hard for me to regret anything I've done. Sometimes I think I ought to be more bummed about what I did. But I wrote some great songs, had a great party in my twenties. I think my biggest regret is anyone I might have influenced to take drugs. I mean, I could blame all the jazz musicians in the forties who made me think heroin was cool. . . ."

"We did a lot of albums fucked up," said Tyler. "*Toys in the Attic* was great. *Rocks* was great. But you can listen to the progression there too. The body gets toxic and the drugs don't work the same way. Even heart patients on digitalis, there's a period after ten or fifteen years where the drug stops working. Same with heroin. The receptors don't get it anymore. It's like a guy at a club and the doorman doesn't recognize him anymore. You can hear that on the albums."

"I think a lot of musicians start getting high because they think it enhances their creativity at first," Tom Hamilton reflected. "[But] after a while it just blows the rest of your brain out, so it doesn't matter. . . . I hate to say so, but when the bass line for 'Sweet Emotion' came into my brain, I'd smoked a joint beforehand. With a musician, anything that makes you approach your instrument differently from the day before can help you come up with new things. . . . [But] you can also do that just by playing a different guitar."

Tyler and Perry even did an anti-drunk-driving spot for Boston's WBZ-TV that began, "We know you're not used to seeing us like this . . ." "We did a concert in Boston against drunk driving," explained Tyler. "The mayor asked us to do it and we said, 'Sure, what the hell.' We were sick and tired of it. It really hurts to see, right after an Aerosmith concert, you get in the limousine and you buzz through the crowd and there's this jam up, some cars smashed, some kids drunk and fucked up, and there's ambulances all over the place. So we went for it. We said, 'We want you alive in '85. Just don't drink while you drive, find a friend to drive you home.'"

However, Aerosmith largely steered away from proselytizing, avoiding music-industry anti-drug campaigns like Rock Against Drugs, which Tim Collins condemned as shallow and hypocritical. "Half of those bands are using drugs! Don't you think the kids know it?" Collins stated. "I say that because I know it firsthand. I can tell you people who I've seen [in Rock Against Drugs spots] on drugs after I've seen them on TV."

"The reason there's so many people strung out [is] because it makes you feel good," Tyler pointed out on radio shock-jock Howard Stern's syndicated show. "That's what's not taught in school. [But] it's dangerous, it's gonna get ya."

Despite the musicians' late-blooming sobriety, other sorts of trouble still dogged them. Leber-Krebs did eventually sue the band, alleging that they broke contracts promising Contemporary Communications five more albums. David Krebs further claimed that he was owed "in the high six-digit figures" for advances already paid to the band. The band countersued, claiming that Leber-Krebs owed *them* money.

In April 1986, Columbia issued *Classics Live,* a motley Krebs-assembled collection of live tracks recorded between 1977 and 1983—some of them rumored to have been punched up with after-the-fact guitar work by Jimmy Crespo and Leber-Krebs client Adam Bomb. The album's main attraction, though, was a previously unreleased studio cut, the Tyler-Perry–written *Rocks* outtake "Major Barbara." When the band protested *Classics Live*'s substandard quality, Krebs claimed the band had been invited to participate in compiling it. To add insult to injury, CBS pushed the rather opportunistic package in *Billboard* with an ad that openly mimicked Geffen's elaborately mounted *Done with Mirrors* campaign.

"I'm not bitter," claimed a bitter-sounding Krebs in *Spin*. "I had twelve good years. It's just rather tragic that we've got outsiders who are tampering with the heart of the band. . . . We're dealing with a group of people who started out as human beings and went through major changes during a period of drug addiction. If you want to know what kind of people Joe Perry and Steven Tyler are, call up their wives and see how much time they've spent with their children lately."

Such talk, it must be said, sounded a mite disingenuous coming from a man who oversaw Aerosmith during its decade-long descent into the depths of addiction.

The band, meanwhile, just seemed happy to be back. "We get so much revitalization from just playing together," Perry told *Creem*. "The audience is there, but we're having such a good time that that's what counts. We're all playing better, [Steven's] singing better, it's been fantastic, and then the audience picks up on it. You see kids out there and they'll absolutely lose their minds. As far as whether we sell out or not, it doesn't matter so much. It matters that you can get the audience off."

The band's next record would do that, and then some.

19

MAGIC TOUCH

The boundary-shattering success of the Run-DMC collaboration was still fresh in the public's mind when the time came for Aerosmith to record its followup to the inconclusive *Done with Mirrors*. The band had actually demoed six rough musical ideas with Rick Rubin in February 1987, but Rubin's schedule didn't allow for the sort of lengthy commitment that an Aerosmith album would require.

The job of producing *Permanent Vacation*—the album that would mark Aerosmith's *real* comeback—fell to Bruce Fairbairn, a well-regarded Canadian whose résumé included work with numerous hard-rocking but commercially savvy bands. By spring, when Aerosmith arrived at Vancouver's Little Mountain Sound to record with Fairbairn, the band had largely conquered its chemical demons and attained some much-needed humility in the process.

The new album's release was preceded in June 1987 by Columbia's release of yet another David Krebs–driven patch-up job, *Classics Live! II,* which was of considerably higher quality than its predecessor thanks to the band's participation. Indeed, the album was far more worthy than its nondescript packaging suggested, with six tracks from the "Back in the Saddle" tour's New Year's Eve, 1984, date at Boston's Orpheum, along with a 1986 version of "Let the Music Do the Talking," recorded at the Centrum in Worcester, and a rendition of "Draw the Line" from 1978's California Jam.

In August, patient fans were rewarded with the genuine article, *Permament Vacation.* Befitting its status as Aerosmith's first official drug-free production, the album was a disciplined, tightly focused effort that found the group sounding more like itself than it had in years. Embodying a remarkably holistic balance of rowdiness and romanticism, of polish and passion, the twelve-song collection made it clear that now Aerosmith was *really* back. Even the band's famed winged logo—AWOL from *Done with Mirrors*—was restored to its rightful place in the album's cover art.

With an eye toward the realities of the contemporary marketplace, John Kalodner had hooked the band—whose songwriting self-sufficiency had previously never been in question—up with renowned song doctors Jim Vallance, Desmond Child, and Holly Knight, who between them had penned mainstream hits for the likes of Kiss, Bon Jovi, and Bryan Adams.

Tyler admitted in *Tower Pulse* that he had initially felt threatened by the suggestion that he work with such hypercommercial tunesmiths. "I thought, 'I don't want to write with these people. It's my music. I'll lose Aerosmith. And I don't want to sound like him.' But what I realized somewhere along the line is that I don't have to . . . If you have a candle, the light won't glow any dimmer if I light yours off of mine. And I certainly don't mind sharing credits. That's not what it's about. It's about writing the definitive song."

The hired guns, writing in various combinations with Tyler and Perry, had a hand in seven of *Permanent Vacation*'s eleven originals, with surprisingly organic-sounding results. The wackily upbeat rocker "Dude (Looks Like a Lady)" and the unsoppily grandiose ballad "Angel," both cowritten by Child, and the brassily humorous "Rag Doll," with compositional tinkerings from Vallance and Knight, constituted a perfect three-way launch for the band's renewed assault on the charts. Child also contributed to the hard-driving opening track "Heart's Done Time," while Vallance lent his expertise to the propulsive "Magic Touch," the lurchingly bluesy "Hangman Jury" and the psychedelipop-flavored "Simoriah."

Whatever one thinks of the outsiders' contributions, *Permanent Vacation* carried an undeniable commercial appeal without losing the spirit of the band's classic work. Likewise, Fairbairn's pristine production, rather than blunting the music's aggression, provided an effective counterbalance to the band's raw attack, while bringing out the best in Tyler's revitalized vocal efforts.

Elsewhere, the horn-driven "Girl Keeps Coming Apart" (featuring part-time trumpet player Fairbairn as part of the six-man Margarita Horns), and the cool, R&B-inflected "St. John," demonstrated that Tyler and Perry could function just fine without the aid of hired hands. Rounding out the program were an enjoyably frantic run through the Lennon-

McCartney raver "I'm Down," and a darkly atmospheric instrumental, "The Movie," which bore the writing credits of all five band members.

As if the expanded scope of *Permanent Vacation*'s musical and lyrical contents wasn't enough, Aerosmith's broadening outlook was also signaled by the inclusion in the credits of *Save the Whales—Support Greenpeace,* a tribute to Hyak and Fina, two killer whales from the Vancouver Aquarium whose songs were featured on "Heart's Done Time."

In contrast to the inconclusive musical and commercial results of *Done with Mirrors, Permanent Vacation* was an across-the-board triumph for Aerosmith, its triple-platinum sales coming as a pleasant surprise even to the band's staunchest supporters. And, in a period when the gap between album-rock success and the pop charts had grown increasingly wide, the disc produced three honest-to-goodness smash singles: the number-3 hit "Angel" and the Top 20–charting "Dude (Looks Like a Lady)" and "Rag Doll."

Meanwhile, the band was finally properly launched into the rock-video era with witty, slickly-produced clips for all three of those hits, which marked the beginning of a fruitful longterm relationship with Kalodner pal Marty Callner, whose snappy visual style made him ideal as their new director of choice. Incidentally, "Dude," the first of the three videos, featured a guest appearance by the flamboyantly bearded Kalodner.

Permanent Vacation's domestic sales were such that a British tour planned for August was cancelled at the last minute to allow Aerosmith to capitalize on its Stateside success. The U.S. tour kicked off in October and found the band making the most of its new lease on life, emerging as a tight, disciplined unit whose consistently impressive performances formed a noticeable contrast to the shabby spectacles that had earlier helped to destroy the band's reputation.

Meanwhile, the once press-shy Tyler seemed intent on using his interviews as a vehicle to exorcise his dark past. Recounting a litany of blown chances and squandered opportunities, Tyler laid out his and his band's physical, spiritual, and fiscal fall from grace in painful detail, estimating that he'd spent over a million dollars on drugs, doing three to five grams of heroin—at $1,000 a gram—per week.

Even the rarely interviewed Joey Kramer spoke enthusiastically of the band's late-blooming maturity. "The benefit now is the support we give to one another," Kramer told *Musician*. "It's a joy to function as a team. If I'm sitting in the back of a limousine twirling my hair and sniffing incessantly, like I do, it doesn't matter. I know those guys love me whatever bullshit comes along. And I feel the same way about them. Those feelings got us here. Everything works when we accept each other as who we are."

"We crawled out from under our problems and got in touch with ourselves," Whitford enthused. "It was a wonderful experience because after all that abuse you go dead inside. You go dead musically, too. Music is such a pure, pure energy. The drugs and alcohol poison your body and take you away from that. Whatever it was when I was a kid that got me so buzzed on music—on the Beatles, on Hendrix—I thought I'd lost that connection. One of the gifts of getting well was rediscovering the power of music, the joy it brings. It's a gift. And to mess with a gift isn't cool. I got a second chance, and it's great."

20

GYPSY BOOTS

The second phase of Aerosmith's second chance moved into second gear with the ten-month tour that followed *Permanent Vacation*. Unlike the "road warp"-inducing marathon odysseys of the band's earlier days, this time around the band took pains to pace itself, heading out on shorter mini-tours, then heading home for a while to recharge, then back out for another spate of shows.

The *Permanent Vacation* shows caught the newly-responsible quintet performing with renewed energy and stamina. The band's old spontaneity seemed to be back, yet the shows were generally steadier and more carefully paced than their sometimes erratic old concerts.

The tour also proved to be Aerosmith's most lucrative to date. "Not only in gross dollars," Collins pointed out to *BAM,* "but in percentage of net to gross, because they didn't waste money. When you're stoned on drugs, or drunk, you don't give a shit about things. Now [that the band members] are in control of themselves, they don't waste money. They don't need a ton of extra people or equipment to validate their self-worth. . . . Today, we only take what we need [on tour]. The band would much rather take the money home than spend it on huge catering or Dom Perignon and all that shit."

One way to cut overhead, Collins discovered, was not to pay for alcohol for the on-the-wagon fivesome's backstage area. "Why should we pay for alcohol for people to come backstage and tempt [the members of Aerosmith], fuck themselves up, and get into a car accident?" reasoned Collins.

And Collins (who had parted ways with partner Barrasso and was now managing the band on his own) was prepared to go to great—some might say extreme—lengths to keep his charges out of temptation's way. The manager had Tyler and Perry taking Antabuse, a pill that causes violent physical reactions if the subject ingests alcohol, and at one point was even collecting urine samples to keep the band honest.

In hotel rooms, Collins had mini-bars emptied of their alcoholic contents before band members' arrivals. The road crew and backstage staffs at each venue were forbidden from consuming alcohol in the band's presence. And instructions were given to the tour's support bands that drugs and alcohol must be kept away from the group at all times. It's also been reported that crew members were fined and even fired after being caught in bars while on tour.

While Aerosmith's anti-alcohol regulations may not have been much of a burden to the *Permanent Vacation* tour's first two opening acts, Dokken and White Lion, it had to have been quite a challenge for the third—budding superstars Guns N'

Roses. Opening for Aerosmith on the tour's third U.S. leg, from July through September 1988 the L.A.-bred Guns N' Roses (who had covered "Mama Kin" on their indie release *Live Like a Suicide*) had been widely acclaimed as inheritors of Aerosmith's roots-conscious bad-boy status.

"They were the first band that really picked up on the way our music actually sounded," Joe Perry raved to *Tower Pulse.* "Just certain things about the way they constructed passages and riffs. Like they listened to Aerosmith and didn't pick up on what we looked like but what we were trying to do musically. They told us that. They made no bones about it and I'm really glad. They're just going from what we did with the Stones and Zeppelin and the Yardbirds. It's no secret. Nobody invented this shit."

Apparently, Aerosmith's influence on Guns N' Roses was more than musical. The cleaned-up 'Smiths must have felt more than a tinge of déjà vu while on tour with the perpetually troubled young combo, whose alcohol and drug intake sharply contrasted the headliners' hard-won sobriety.

Understandably, Tim Collins had insisted that the opening acts' standard tour contracts ban alcohol from the backstage area, but for Guns N' Roses he made a partial exception. "We made a deal with them," Collins explained to *BAM.* "We told them we wouldn't pay for any of their drugs or alcohol—we didn't want to enable their activities. But if they chose to [use drugs], they could do that in their dressing room."

Still, Guns N' Roses' stint on the tour (which included a show at New Jersey's 63,000-seat Giants Stadium, where the bill also included U.K. metal legends Deep Purple) saw the petulant youngsters living up to their rep for volatility. Despite the temperamental gulf between the clean-and-sober

Aerosmith and the cruisin'-for-a-bruisin' Guns N' Roses, the members of Aerosmith responded to the Gunners' exploits like worldlier big brothers rather than judgmental parents.

According to Collins, the members of both bands "have become incredibly good friends. Aerosmith, though they've chosen to let go of drugs and alcohol, understand totally where the guys in Guns N' Roses are at. It's like looking in a mirror." As for the Gunners' chances of cleaning up their act, Collins predicted, "Those guys have to do about two million dollars' worth of dope before they're ready for recovery."

Despite their much-publicized cleanup efforts, Aerosmith tended to avoid preaching about their sobriety. "I don't push my shit on anybody. I don't say, 'You're an asshole for using drugs,'" Tyler told *Musician.* "There's a time and a place for it. You don't go backstage and brag about your time. You just try to pass it on. Tell them how hard it is, how beautiful it is. I tell them there's a whole world of music out there, and they're living in a cave with a boulder at the door, and the boulder is drugs. You kick the boulder out of the way, you can go in and out, invite your friends in."

"We never preach," said Collins. "People are gonna do what they're gonna do. We can only show by example. All I can say is, if you look at a band like Aerosmith, they were at a low point in their career, they gave up drugs and alcohol, they started working to better themselves—and their multiplatinum career is back. It's not a coincidence."

With their careers back on track, the band members could better enjoy their stable, settled family lives. Teresa Barrick, Tyler's longtime girlfriend and designer of his flamboyant stage costumes, became his third wife on May 28, 1988, and would give birth to his second daughter, Chelsea Anna, the following year, with a son, Taj, to follow. Perry was now married to his second wife Billie; between them they had three children, Adrian from Joe's first marriage, Aaron from Billie's first and Joe and Billie's son Anthony. Brad Whitford and his second wife Karen were the parents of a son, Zachary. The childless Tom and Terry Hamilton were still together, their marriage having withstood all manner of trials. And Joey Kramer and his wife, April, were the parents of son Jesse Sky, as well as raising Asia, April's daughter from her first marriage.

The release of *Permanent Vacation* was followed by the release of no less than three home-video packages spotlighting the band. While *3 x 5* was a compilation of the album's three promo clips, *Video Scrapbook* was a more rewarding, hourlong collection of concert performances and candid footage. In October, Sony exhumed footage of the band's decade-old (and decidedly lackluster) Dallas Cotton Bowl performance as the longform home video *Live Texxas Jam.*

The same month saw Columbia again exercise its contractual prerogative to cobble together another best-of collection, *Gems,* whose ostensible purpose was to collect such "hardrock AOR tracks" as "Rats in the Cellar," "Mama Kin," "Critical Mass," "Lord of the Thighs," and "Train Kept A Rollin'," and which did have the added virtue of the previously unreleased studio version of "Chip Away the Stone."

Whatever annoyance the band might have felt with these blatantly exploitative packages was probably overshadowed by the success that had inspired their release.

Easy street. (*Larry Busacca/Retna*)

21

DON'T GET MAD, GET EVEN

By the end of the 1980s, Aerosmith had not only solidified a startling commercial comeback, but were also beginning to achieve the critical cachet which they'd long sought. As Ira Robbins observed in *Newsday,* "Time cuts two ways for Aerosmith. When the hard-rocking quintet first roared out of Boston in the early seventies, so much of its look, sound, and stance was borrowed from the Rolling Stones that no serious consideration of Aerosmith as a truly world-class rock 'n' roll band could be entertained. Despite massive success, Aerosmith was defined by its class roots as a second-generation derivative. By the end of the decade, even that position was untenable. Drug-addled and dissipated, the group splintered and collapsed. Aerosmith's youth and time had both run out.

"Ironically," Robbins continued, "as groups like Led Zeppelin and the Rolling Stones also discovered, years of inactivity only fanned the flames of legend. While sitting on the sidelines, Aerosmith grew from has-been joke to top-rank myth. For a new generation of young fans raised on classic-rock radio, the chicken-or-egg aspect of Aerosmith's origins was as irrelevant as the five-year age difference between Steven Tyler and Mick Jagger."

Nowhere was the irony of the band's new status as dignified elder statesmen more apparent than in the film documentary *The Decline of Western Civilization Part II: The Metal Years,* in which director Penelope Spheeris juxtaposed Aerosmith's hard-won insights with the reckless behavior of their younger acolytes—a contrast that would have been unthinkable to anyone who'd known Aerosmith during their debauched heyday a few years earlier.

By the time the band finished touring behind *Permanent Vacation,* it was time to start thinking about a new album. They'd already accumulated a healthy backlog of musical ideas for the next disc—which Tyler at one point threatened to title *Bobbing for Piranhas,* but which ended up bearing the simpler but more memorable moniker of *Pump* when it was released in September 1989.

It was with an attitude of serious professionalism that the band returned to Little Mountain Studios where, coincidentally, Mötley Crüe was also recording. The year before, the Crüe's bassist Nikki Sixx had been befriended and sponsored by Tyler for Alcoholics Anonymous after Sixx narrowly survived a heroin overdose. Members of both bands spent much of their free time together, jogging, working out, and going out to strip joints.

Tom Hamilton later revealed that it wasn't until the *Pump* sessions that he completely embraced sobriety. "I was the last one in the band to get it," he told *Musician*. "During *Permanent Vacation* I wasn't drinking but I was smoking a bowl of pot every day. I'd get to rehearsal and Steven would look me in the eyes and say, 'Hey!' It was stupid on my part. My mental energy was going into remembering the arrangements instead of playing what I felt like playing. Eventually I got sick of being paranoid, of being the only one out there. My priorities were wrong. On *Pump* I finally played what I felt because I had the arrangements down cold."

Pump also found Hamilton reexploring his instrumental technique, taking bass lessons while immersing himself in the work of such influential players as Led Zeppelin's John Paul Jones and legendary Motown bassist James Jamerson. "In fact, I overdid it and ended up with an inflamed tendon in my ring finger," he recalled. "When I find something I can't play, I tend to practice it until there are flames in my forearms."

Joey Kramer, meanwhile, worked with Hamilton to sharpen the songs' grooves. "No one could accuse me of overplaying," Kramer said, "and on this album I tried to make it even simpler, concentrate on making the grooves happen. I'm concerned with improving myself and making the band sound as good as it can sound."

"Joey and I ended up practicing a lot together to work out the details," said Hamilton. "That's something we always said we were going to do, but this time we actually did it."

Musically, *Pump* more or less picked up where *Permanent Vacation* left off, further mining Aerosmith's trademark mix of aggression, melody, and lyrical wit, while venturing into more exotic and off-center areas. The latter quality manifested itself in the interludes of tribal chants, bizarre instrumental snippets, and risqué spoken-word bits that linked *Pump*'s songs, adding a welcome twisted edge to the songs' effortless accessibility.

Tyler had first gotten the idea for the album's between-song oddities after listening to one of Guns N' Roses guitarist Izzy Stradlin's esoteric tapes of ethnic music. "I made a list of all the instruments I ever wanted on an album but didn't have," he said, "tubas following the bassline, kazoos following the lead guitar lines, backwards drums—just weird ideas and instruments."

For the occasion, the band sought the assistance of Randy Raine Reusch, a Vancouver-based collector of ethnic instruments from around the world. "Joe and I went to his place and tried everything," said Tyler. "Except the drum made out of a human skull. We didn't want the karma. I didn't want to be banging away on some P.O.W. We did try all the other instruments and used the good stuff.

"I'd already put together the chant at the beginning of 'Voodoo Medicine Man,'" Tyler continued. "That's Zulu virgin girls, hundreds of them, stomping their feet with bells on, doing their rites before they get poked by these guys. It all started to fit together, became thematic, became a thing of itself. And if people don't like the in-between stuff, they can program it out on CD. The songs are great."

Indeed, *Pump*'s more eclectic elements didn't overshadow the flawless commercial savvy that had made *Permanent Vacation* such a decisive turn in the band's fortunes. Maintaining the prior album's irresistible commercial edge, *Pump,* whose cover bore a simple but oddly elegant pic of two trucks engaged in a sexually suggestive pose, gracefully balanced serious lyrical content, sonic adventurousness, and sheer rocking abandon—standing as an impressive testament to Aerosmith's eternal youth *and* its thoughtful adulthood.

Desmond Child and Jim Vallance again contributed their radio-friendly expertise on two tracks each, and Tyler and Perry seemed to have grown a bit more comfortable with the idea of working with outside songwriting collaborators. "We try not to get caught up in trends, but we're not afraid to try new things, either," said Perry. "We never say, 'Aerosmith shouldn't sound like this.' We're not afraid to put our egos aside. Being brought to our knees by drugs made us realize that we don't have all the answers."

"I think 'Let the Music Do the Talking' was the definitive Aerosmith song. But it didn't do shit. And about that, I'm angry," Tyler said to *Tower Pulse.* "[But] I can be angry from now until my dick grows another four inches and it just won't happen. You gotta put a couple of appetizers, a couple of teasers, to wet their thing. And I'm embarrassed that I have to play that game. . . . But I also want to be loved. I want to be heard. It's like, I know that if the Beatles hadn't put out a 'She Loves You,' they wouldn't have been able to put out a 'Penny Lane' or any of the sideways stuff they did."

"Young Lust" kick-started *Pump* on a note of frantic, crotch-driven urgency, and the raving "F.I.N.E." (an acronym for "fucked-up, insecure, neurotic, and emotional") demonstrated that Tyler's knack for risqué lyricism hadn't been dimmed by his newly cleaned-up lifestyle. The same held true for "Love in an Elevator," which matched one of Tyler's most sex-obsessed lyrics (apparently based on a true story) with one of the band's most insistent choruses.

From those powerful odes to abandon, the album

moved to more serious matters. The pulsing "Monkey on My Back" found Tyler dealing forthrightly with his addiction problem, while "Janie's Got a Gun" unflinchingly took on the touchy topic of child abuse, combining a memorable hook with a brutally frank lyric dealing with father-daughter incest and its harrowing aftermath, its lyrics reportedly inspired by the true story of a girl who shot her abusive father to death.

The remainder of *Pump* continued in a relatively light-hearted vein, with the band in typically rocking form. The bracing lurcher "The Other Side," featuring the Margarita Horns in overdrive, was perhaps the band's most satisfying venture into R&B territory to date. "My Girl" and "Don't Get Mad, Get Even" caught Tyler in swaggering-smartass mode, while "Voodoo Medicine Man" offered an atmospheric slice of jungle fever. And "What It Takes" ended the album on a note of gratifying balladic uplift.

"Basically we're working the songs the same way we did when we got the band together," Joe Perry told *Musician.* "On *Done with Mirrors* we tried to write in the studio. We always felt that Steven wrote best under pressure—at least that's how we did it for years. But [on] the best albums, we had all the songs done before we went in and recorded them. If you leave some space, you can write in the studio, but you have to have the framework.

"There's different things to do for inspiration," said Perry. "On 'My Girl' Steven played the drums when we were writing, but on 'Elevator' he played a keyboard. . . . One night we saw Keith Richards and he did 'Connection.' That got us thinking about all the classic English rock songs from the sixties, and the next day we wrote 'My Girl.' On 'Don't Get Mad, Get Even,' I wrote the music before Steven even came in.

Two generations of swagger, Steven Tyler and Jon Bon Jovi.
(*Kevin Statham/S.I.N.*)

"Every day when we go in to write we try to get something on cassette. Just so we wrote something. So when I go home I can prove to my wife I've been at the studio playing. One of those days when I didn't have anything inspired, I took 'Rag Doll' and listened to it backwards. The chords just hit me and I started playing 'Don't Get Mad.' Steven heard it the next day and wrote the lyrics."

Upon its September 1989 release, *Pump* followed in *Permanent Vacation*'s multiplatinum footsteps (it ended up selling over four million), notching a diverse trio of audio/video hits in "Love in an Elevator," "Janie's Got a Gun," and "The Other Side," while receiving uniformly enthusiastic reviews. The album was eventually joined on the retail racks by two long-form home-video packages, *The Making of Pump* and *Things That Go Pump in the Night*.

The band hit the road the month after the album's release. With hired hand Thom Gimbel rounding out the sound on keyboards and sax, Aerosmith began an honest-to-goodness (if brief) European tour, encompassing dates in Germany, Italy, France, Belgium, the Netherlands, Scandinavia, and Britain—commencing with an electrifying November 14 show at London's Hammersmith Odeon. The Hammersmith show—on which Whitesnake frontman David Coverdale joined the band for an encore rendition of "I'm Down"—was a raging success, erasing bad memories of the band's disastrous prior assaults on the U.K. market.

Back in the States, Aerosmith launched the first leg of its U.S. tour on December 15, with fast-rising Jersey rockers Skid Row as the opening act—once again demonstrating that they weren't afraid to share the stage with hot young competitors. The East Coast trek continued in wildly successful fashion, including the by-now routine three-night stand at Boston Garden. The tour's overwhelmingly upbeat vibe was marred only by an incident at the Civic Center in Springfield, Massachusetts, where Skid Row frontman Sebastian Bach was arrested and charged with assault and battery after jumping into the crowd mid-set to search out the fan who'd beaned him with a bottle.

By now, Aerosmith's touring regimen had been eased by the addition of a rented Cessna Citation private jet, formerly belonging to deposed Philippine dictator Ferdinand Marcos, which the band had temporarily christened "Aeroforce One." The plane was an extravagance perhaps, but with two consecutive blockbuster albums restoring the group to rock's fast track, the indulgence, for once, seemed earned.

The U.S. tour's second leg—on which the band was accompanied by soon-to-be-huge seventies revivalists the Black Crowes—was followed in June by a trip to New York during which the band picked up a couple of International Rock Awards, and performed as special guests at guitar legend Les Paul's celebrity-studded 75th birthday party. The month climaxed with a mammoth show at Toronto's 62,000-capacity National Exhibition Center, with Metallica, Warrant, and the Black Crowes rounding out the bill.

By the time the fourth and final U.S. leg of the tour closed at the end of July, Aerosmith was listed as the second-highest-grossing touring band in the U.S. (second only to the Rolling Stones, appropriately enough), having played for more than 1,750,000 American fans and racking up twenty-five million dollars' worth of ticket sales on the *Pump* tour.

The band spent much of August and September in Europe as "Special Guest" on the Monsters of Rock tour, performing in front of an audience of eighty thousand at

England's Donington Park on August 18, on a bill that also included Whitesnake and Poison. At that show, long-time idol Jimmy Page came onstage to jam on "Train Kept A Rollin'." The Donington extravaganza was followed two days later by a not-so-secret "secret" club gig at London's legendary Marquee, climaxed by Page's reappearance for a six-song encore.

In September, Aerosmith took home three MTV Video Music Awards. That honor was followed by a belated return trip to Japan (no word of whether turkey was served backstage), the band's first-ever visit to Australia, and another round of U.S. shows.

By the time all the bodies were counted, *Pump* had sold over four million copies, the band had won a Best Rock Performance Grammy for "Janie's Got a Gun," along with American Music Awards as Favorite Band and Favorite Heavy Metal Artist, and a Rolling Stone Reader's Poll nod as Best American Band.

Not a bad year for a bunch of former has-beens.

22

THE HAND THAT FEEDS

As if Aerosmith's commercial resurgence and late-blooming respectability weren't enough to confound the expectations of longtime observers, the nineties saw the veteran rockers assume an equally unexpected new role—that of responsible political spokesmen.

The band's emerging social conscience first asserted itself in the *Pump* hit "Janie's Got a Gun," whose implicit female-empowerment message made it clear that the band's five eternal teenagers—now forty-something husbands and dads—had been doing some serious thinking about some serious adult matters. While Steven Tyler bristled at the press's suggestions that it was the first Aerosmith song to tackle a serious issue, he admitted that the issue of child abuse had got to him.

"Maybe it was on my mind because of that *Newsweek*

cover about everyone who had been murdered in a week," Tyler told *Musician*. "What I know about child abuse is that we all go through three phases: 1) when you get shit from your parents; 2) when you realize you got shit from your parents and you swear you'll never do it to your own kids; and 3) when you give shit to your own kids because you forgot what your parents did."

"Janie's Got a Gun" was particularly remarkable in light of the hard-rock genre's standard patronizing portrayal of women—a sin of which Aerosmith had not been entirely blameless in the past, although their transgressions in this area had generally been executed with a bit more flair and wit than most of their peers. "Men are too busy talking about how big our dicks are," said Tyler, who'd been spotted wearing a T-shirt with the slogan IF MEN BLED, TAMPONS WOULD BE FREE. "Obviously women are the superior sex."

The singer even seemed to take a more thoughtful view of Aerosmith's more traditional lyrical subject matter. When asked by *Musician* writer Charles M. Young what he'd tell a PMRC (Parents Music Resource Center—the anti-rock watchdog group cofounded by future Second Lady Tipper Gore) mom who objected to her daughter hearing a song like "Young Lust," Tyler responded, "Well, she's coming at her daughter's life from the wrong direction. How can you fight young lust?—a) she's young, and b) she has lust. That's why people masturbate. I mean, what do you want to be telling your child? That lust is bad? Get outta here. That's the Holy Wars."

In the same article, Joe Perry acknowledged his songwriting partner's expanding horizons: "Every year his lyrical concerns open up a little more. As we're getting sober, the windows open and you see other things out there. They say that whatever age you are when you first take a drink, that's the mental age you are when you stop. He's working on twenty-two right now. By the time he's sixty, he might be almost normal."

"We've done songs with messages," Perry observed. "More are creeping in. But if it's preachy, I don't want to hear it."

Aerosmith's newfound social responsibility also asserted itself through a number of extramusical activities, revealing an activist passion that made it clear just how far the quintet's collective consciousness had expanded since their days as rock's most notorious hedonists. The band helped raise twenty tons' worth of groceries on a drive for a Boston food bank, performed a benefit show at the Las Vegas Hard Rock Cafe to benefit a local center for abused women, and was featured in a clever TV spot for the Rock the Vote campaign. Perry, meanwhile, was often spotted playing a blonde Schecter guitar emblazoned with the slogan "Protest and Survive."

But Aerosmith's most passionate efforts in the sociopolitical arena involved free-speech issues, obviously an issue dear to the habitually outspoken band's heart. In the spring of 1992, the band emerged as leaders in a growing artistic-community groundswell against the National Endowment for the Arts, whose increasingly philistine policies were beginning to strike many observers as bordering on censorship. At a press conference at the List Visual Arts Center in Cambridge, Massachusetts, the band handed over a check for $10,000 to support "Corporal Politics," an exhibition of sexually explicit photographs whose federal grant for the same amount had been vetoed by the NEA. Aerosmith's gesture earned the attention of *Time* magazine, which labeled its story "Rock to the Rescue."

With typically blunt aplomb, Tyler stated the case for the band's acts on behalf of the First Amendment.

"Rock 'n' roll is about a backbeat you can fuck to, but it's also about saying 'fuck you' to people who don't get off on freedom. We're protecting our right to rock."

Later, when Aerosmith guested on NBC-TV's *Saturday Night Live*, Tyler acknowledged the network's earlier refusal to air the risqué "Love in an Elevator" video by singing "Get that fuckin' monkey off my back" during the band's performance of "Monkey on My Back." (That was about as serious as the show got. On the same *SNL* episode, the band members were featured as themselves in a "Wayne's World" sketch, bantering with regulars Dana Carvey and Mike Myers on Wayne and Garth's basement set. Later, the 'Smiths—and John Kalodner—would be featured as cartoon characters on an episode of *The Simpsons*.)

In a story published in *Newsday*, Perry articulated the band's common-sense approach to free-speech issues. "I don't want my six-year-old kid watching MTV at eight in the morning, but I don't want some government agency telling me I can't let him."

Tom Hamilton agreed, stating "I respect anybody who says, 'I'm scared about the amount of violence and sexual exploitation on TV.' But not when they go on to, 'Everybody should think like me, and if they don't we're going to use our power to propose laws to get everybody to agree.'"

"The secret to enlightenment is to lighten up," philosophized Tyler. "Whether you're talking rock 'n' roll or women, the fever's what it's about. The band has the fever. We're all here because we're not all there."

Tyler's personalized hybrid of adult introspection and childish mischief continued to make great copy. As veteran music journalist Charles M. Young observed in *Musician*, "Conversing with Tyler is like interviewing a volcano. He doesn't so much

Wayne's World! Wayne's World! Party On! Excellent! (*Warner Brothers Records*)

talk as erupt with a molten spew of extended and usually mixed metaphors, pungent homilies and physical ob-
servations of striking immediacy ('Look at those tits!'). He often
speaks of the need to let the creative child inside him come out to
play, while it seems vastly more probable that it is the adult who
is chained and flogged in the dank recesses of his unconscious."

Or, as Hamilton noted, "His brain has much more capacity to be obsessed with sex now that he's not fucked up."

Perry admitted that being Tyler's partner can be exhaust-
ing, but added, "I also love being with him. We're spending
more time together than we've ever spent. When we were doing
the album, we took off with our families and rented a couple of
cabins together for a break. There are times I don't see him for
days, too. I think I make my boundaries better than he does, and
that's why we work well together. He's putting out a stream of
stuff, and the job becomes to steer it the right way."

In fact, it now seemed as if Tyler and Perry's often contentious partnership had arrived at some sort of mature resolu-
tion, with the two principals learning to accept and embrace
each other's quirks. "To this day, he still wears a lot of armor,"
Tyler says of Perry, "but music was always the saving grace. And
if that's the way he chooses to let me in, that's fine. I just need to
keep coming up with my own passwords to get in there."

"He's so intuitive that at first when we were using drugs it
helped," Perry notes. "The trick now is to keep it flowing whatever happens, then worry about what's good and bad after it's
down on the tape. . . . For years I thought he was at his wittiest
just sitting around talking, and when he tried to write the log-
jam started to build. He's one of the funniest people I know, and
every album now he's getting closer to laying it down so we can
use it."

"I don't question it. It just flows," Tyler said of the band's resurgent creative process. "I used to think, 'Well, I'll just snort some Xanax and write the lyrics.' Psychologically it was a wasteland. Now, it's like this book I was reading by Og Mandino: 'Persist,' he said. 'Persist, until you drop, but persist.' He told this parable about a guy who had a tree in front of his house and a tiny hatchet. Every day he took one swipe. In a month that tree was down. . . . But you can't see that unless you *do* it.

"You set up a time and you be there," Tyler said. "It's as simple as that. Joe and I keep the tape rolling and for six hours we pound away. Then we bring the tape home and we mark it down. One-dash-one, that was 'Monkey on My Back.' I sat behind the drums, I got a good bass sound, and I let the kid out totally. I let my head fly. I sing what Joe tells me with his guitar. Music is a language. The sound is an afterproduct. Minor is sad, major is happy—that's the basis for a conversation, isn't it? If I listen closely, I hear Joe talking to me, and I sing. I don't know where it comes from. I like to think of myself as a channel."

By now, Aerosmith's rehabilitation had gotten so much attention that even Steven Tyler claimed to have had enough. "I'm getting tired of recovery stories," he told *Musician,* before adding, "I can look you in the eye and tell you I'm a miracle. I didn't have a drink today, and I did drink for twenty-seven years. I shot coke and heroin, and for the last three years I haven't had anything more powerful than an aspirin. I went to four rehabs before it took.

"The great thing about Aerosmith is not only the instant gratification of going onstage, but you can see yourself get sober on the albums—the musical difference when we were using, when we were using just a little, when we first got sober, and now. You can chart it."

The biggest mouth in the biz. (*CREDIT TK/S.I.N.*)

23

GOTTA LOVE IT

Columbia commemorated its re-signing of Aerosmith with the November 1991 release of *Pandora's Box,* a smartly-assembled, lavishly packaged three-CD boxed set of greatest hits and assorted oddities.

The previously unreleased goodies included in-concert versions of "Write Me a Letter," "Walkin' the Dog," "Lord of the Thighs," "I Wanna Know Why," " Big Ten Inch Record," "Adam's Apple," "Kings and Queens," "Chip Away the Stone," and "Rattlesnake Shake," alternate studio versions of "Movin' Out" and "Major Barbara," and studio-recorded covers of Otis Rush's blues standard "All Your Love" and the Beatles' "Helter Skelter." Also of historical interest were "South Station Blues" from the second Joe Perry Project album, the Whitford/St. Holmes track "Sharpshooter," and "When I Needed You," a 1966 tune by Tyler's prehistoric combo Chain Reaction.

Of even greater interest to rabid Aerofans, though, were the samplings of the band's casual studio jams, usually featuring Tyler on keyboards, which offered a tantalizing glimpse into the band's creative workings. For example, the 1975 "Soul Saver" later evolved into "Nobody's Fault," which followed it on the boxed set, and 1979's "Let It Slide" eventually became "Cheese Cake."

In March of 1993, *Us* magazine reported that notorious sex maniac Tyler had entered a twelve-step marital-fidelity program. "My idea of sexuality is so warped and twisted," he confessed. "I went away to a place for sexual concerns because I thought I was a sex addict. Back when I was getting high, I didn't fuck around with women. For a while, I was really pissed off that I'd missed those fruits because I was stoned in a closet somewhere, snorting blow with whoever. I thought that I was owed something—'Now that I'm sober, I deserve to get laid.'"

Tyler revealed one of his new tactics for staying faithful. "Every time I get the feeling that I want to fool around with some other woman, I pretend that my wife is in the room."

During a visit to Howard Stern's radio show, Tyler and Perry insisted that their days of on-the-road hanky-panky are over. "Murphy's law's been followin' us around for years, and I would be the one rock star that you'd see on the cover of the [*New York*] *Post*," laughed Tyler.

Spring 1993 saw Aerosmith release its eleventh studio album, *Get a Grip*, which, to no one's surprise, was another instant smash—even if its computer-fabricated cover shot of a cow's udder pierced by an earring did little to endear the band to certain animal-rights activists.

The making of *Get a Grip* (with Bruce Fairbairn again behind the production desk) was a lengthy but ultimately rewarding process, with work beginning in early 1992 at L.A.'s A&M Studios. It was during those sessions that the band came up with the five songs that form *Get a Grip*'s musical and conceptual core: "Eat the Rich," "Get a Grip," "Fever," "Crazy," and "Amazing." "We basically made a whole record there except for the mixing," Perry told *Rolling Stone*. "But we decided the songs just didn't jump, and we had to keep going."

The group had originally intended to record another two or three songs to add to the A&M tracks, but once Tyler and Perry returned to Perry's home studio (affectionately dubbed "the Boneyard") and started kicking ideas around, they came up with, in Tyler's words, "a shitload of great stuff" and decided that they "had to make it the biggest, the baddest, the bravest and the scariest Aerosmith record yet."

The band returned home to do some more writing and then returned to Little Mountain Studios, where they laid down "Livin' on the Edge," "Flesh," "Walk On Down," "Shut Up and Dance," "Cryin'," "Gotta Love It," "Line Up," and "Boogie Man." Said Tyler of the album's lengthy gestation period, "It feels like a long time, but the longer it takes the better it feels."

With the aid of the Digital Audio Tape (DAT) medium, elements of the songs' early rough demos made it to the album's final mix. "The reason why we do that," according to Tyler, "is because when something goes down and Joe goes, 'What did you say, Steven?' and I go, 'I don't know,' we're able to turn the tape back. With DAT tape you can keep it rolling for up to eight hours, I think, on the slow speeds. It's like, tape's rolling, you're burning. . . . You have that tape and we can fly it in, which is a beautiful thing. We did it on four songs."

The choice of Atlanta-based producer/engineer/ musician Brendan O'Brien (the sonic architect—and purported ghost musician—behind the Black Crowes' success) to mix the album gave the songs a grittier, down-and-dirty atmosphere that echoed the hard-headed insistence of the band's esteemed seventies classics. Or, as Tyler said, "Sounds like a good fuck."

Once again, Tyler and Perry drew on the talents of several outside songwriting collaborators, including familiar faces Desmond Child (who cowrote the surging stroll "Crazy" and the steamy "Flesh"), Jim Vallance (the jungle speed-metal "Eat the Rich" and the sassily self-deflating title track), and Richie Supa (the uplifting redemption ode "Amazing"), as well as new acquaintances Mark Hudson (the tensely jangly "Livin' on the Edge" and the vaguely surreal "Gotta Love It"), Lenny Kravitz (the infectiously R&B-laced "Line Up"), and Damn Yankees members Jack Blades and Tommy Shaw (the slyly driving semi-rap "Shut Up and Dance").

Elsewhere, Perry sang the sadder-but-wiser lyrics of his solo composition "Walk On Down," which, like "Get a Grip" and "Fever," seemed to allude lyrically to the band's prior problems. "Honestly, I didn't get it on the first couple of listens," Tyler said of the former tune, "but I heard it again and thought, 'That's fucking great!' It's a staunch fucking thing, y'know? Plus, it gives me time to take a piss in the middle of the show!"

On the more sensitive side, the tightly-wound "Livin' on the Edge" and the grandly uplifting "Amazing" delivered unforced messages of social tension and spiritual transcendence. "Crazy" and the soulful stroll "Cryin'" showed off Aerosmith's unexpected knack for heart-on-sleeve balladry.

"It's a gift, and if it's a gift why shouldn't I use it?" Tyler said of the band's new status as pop romantics. "Don't be afraid that it'll sound like the Everly Brothers. It's not them. It's you. When I do 'Cryin'' and put all those harmonies on top of it—in the early days I would have left that off. Now I stick more of that on and you're hearing more of Steven's voice. I'm not afraid of that anymore."

But the hook-intensive *Get a Grip*'s most impressive feat, perhaps, was the fact that this group of millionaire rock stars managed not to sound like self-satisfied hypocrites on a song called "Eat the Rich."

According to Tyler, *Get a Grip*'s title refers to the topical focus of several of the album's songs. "This is how we feel about what's going on and this is what it sounds like," he said. "You have to grab hold. Sometimes it's your crotch, sometimes it's reality. I'm still screaming about what's inside me but now a lot of that relates to what's happening in the world outside. Everybody likes to blame shit on everybody else so they don't have to own up to it themselves. But sooner or later it hits you upside the head—unless you get a grip."

Still, Tyler carried no high-handed illusions about Aerosmith's mission. "We know we're not a message band," he told *Newsday*. "We know people like to . . . throw back a bunch of beers, have fun and forget the rest of the world. That's the premise around Aerosmith."

But don't these married, middle-aged dads ever feel tempted to write about their lives as responsible parents? "We write songs about making children, not raising them," Perry responded.

Despite *Get a Grip*'s multiplatinum success—selling five million copies in the U.S. and an additional five million overseas—the critics weren't quite as unanimously enthusiastic as they'd been about the album's two immediate predecessors. *Rolling Stone*'s Mark Coleman viewed *Get a Grip* as a safely formulaic regression from the lofty aesthetic heights achieved on *Permanent Vacation* and *Pump*. "If 'Janie's Got a Gun' opened possibilities for this group and hard rock in general, the formulaic macho slobber of 'Flesh' and the humorless clean-living uplift of 'Livin' on the Edge' slam them shut," Coleman wrote.

Still, Coleman acknowledged that Aerosmith's effortless expertise still shone through. "Playing together as a band for twenty-odd years definitely has its advantages; each instrumental voice distinctly holds its own in an instantly recognizable blend."

When Aerosmith played Long Island's Jones Beach Theater in September 1993, *Newsday*'s Ira Robbins acknowledged the meticulously crafted spectacle of the two-hour set, but felt that the band was "going through the motions." But when the group returned to play at New York City's Madison Square Garden the following February, Robbins was considerably more impressed.

"Whatever it is that fuels Aerosmith's unforgettable fire after all these years (carrot juice? pasta? milk of magnesia?) must have been plentifully stocked backstage," Robbins wrote, "because the veteran band was neither feeling nor showing its age. . . . This was primal rock and roll in full effect, a top-notch spectacle by masters of the craft. For all of Steven Tyler's flowing finery and exaggerated theatrics (nobody in rock can simulate sex with more panache), and the band's current reliance on ambitious video narratives, the aging Aerosmith is still, at its impossibly skinny and lithe heart, a stripped-down rock band that can lace up its own songs onstage."

In September of 1993, Sony/Columbia—with the band's participation—began one of the most extensive catalogue-restoration projects in rock history, simultaneously issuing repackaged, sonically upgraded CD versions of the band's twelve Columbia releases—*Aerosmith, Get Your Wings, Toys in the Attic, Rocks, Draw the Line, Live Bootleg, Night in the Ruts, Greatest Hits, Rock in a Hard Place, Classics Live!, Classics Live! II,* and *Gems.* In addition to featuring supposedly superior "Super-Bit Mastering," the new discs were issued with expanded limited-edition artwork featuring photos and memorabilia from the respective periods of the albums' original releases. The upgraded reissues were later repackaged in the massive *Box of Fire,* which combined the dozen Columbia albums with a bonus disc containing five rare tracks not included on *Pandora's Box.*

The refurbishing of the Aerosmith CD catalogue was the first tangible by-product of the band's return to Sony, finally giving the band control over how its back catalogue was packaged and sold—an issue which didn't seem nearly as important when they signed their first record deal.

"That shit didn't really matter to us in the early days," Perry told *Pulse.* "We never thought it was gonna matter if we had control over our fuckin' catalogue 'cause we thought we'd be dead. Who knew? But now we've realized that all that is really important. Christ, every time they change a format, y'know, you've got to be there to make sure they don't screw up the mixes or the mastering."

Meanwhile, Aerosmith's presence on MTV was stronger than ever, thanks to director Marty Callner's consistently inventive visualizations of "Livin' on the Edge," "Crazy," and "Amazing." In an interesting bit of intergenerational strangeness, the "Crazy" clip starred Tyler's sixteen-year-old daughter Liv as one of a pair of teen nymphettes. Oddly, though, Tyler reportedly attempted to prevent *Interview* magazine from identifying him as the father of the teenager when it ran a photo of him with rising actress/model Liv, who was later seen smooching suggestively on the cover with her old man on the cover of *Rolling Stone*. (Liv, the oldest of Tyler's four offspring, is the sole progeny of his liaison with Bebe Buell, who during her pregnancy had split with Tyler and relocated to Maine.)

The Japanese leg of the *Get a Grip* tour saw a last-minute substitution in the Aerosmith lineup when Brad Whitford had to miss two dates in order to fly home to attend to a family illness. Stepping into the guitarist's shoes for those shows was Boston alternative-rock stalwart Dave Minehan, former leader of the critically acclaimed Neighborhoods, whose 1990 album *Hoodwinked* Whitford coproduced.

Get a Grip's on-again, off-again eighteen-month roadshow culminated in the summer of 1994 with the band's headlining appearance at the Monsters of Rock show in Donington Park, on a bill that included such young upstarts as Pantera, Extreme, Sepultura, Therapy?, Cry of Love, and Biohazard, followed by an even more newsworthy appearance at the two-day Woodstock '94 anniversary show.

As if those appearances weren't sufficient evidence of Aerosmith's status as rock-culture icons, in the wake of Nirvana leader (and heroin addict) Kurt Cobain's suicide, Tim Collins publicly called for major labels to set up special departments to help artists deal with drug-related problems. Speaking to the music-industry trade magazine *Billboard,* Collins said that he'd been inspired to make the statement by Tyler's anger over Cobain's death.

"Almost nobody gives these people any direction, or even any information on how to live with themselves," said Collins. "Cobain's tragic end is symptomatic of the sickness in our industry and in the greater American culture itself," Collins stated; adding, "The industry always spends so much money on technology—making the music sound better. Why not spend some on helping the creators of the music stay alive and thrive? We're killing our artists for short-term greed."

At the 1994 Grammy Awards, Aerosmith performed "Livin' on the Edge," which won for Best Performance by a Duo or Group but lost out in the Best Rock Song stakes to Soul Asylum's "Runaway Train." They later picked up a trio of MTV Video Music Awards, including a Best Video nod for "Cryin'." And at Boston's Pepsi Music Awards, where the group picked up its seventh consecutive award as Outstanding Rock Band, they were also given a Right to Rock award in recognition of their pro–First Amendment activities, presented to the band by famed defense attorney Alan Dershowitz.

On a lighter but no less significant note, in June 1994 Aerosmith made its video-game debut as the stars of *Revolution X,* whose futuristic premise pitted the players against a military-industrial organization that's kidnapped the members of Aerosmith as part of a plot to control the world's youth. The game's players, armed with a weapon that fires deadly sharpened CDs at the bad guys, are called upon to travel to various exotic locations in order to rescue the band. Along with specially-shot video footage of the band, the game incorporated "Eat the Rich," "Sweet Emotion," "Toys in the Attic," and "Walk This Way" into its storyline.

According to George Petro, one of *Revolution X's* codesigners, "We wanted the band to serve as the wise elders that guide players through the game. Aerosmith was perfect because they've been there and back. They've already been through the fire and come out stronger."

In July the band plunged further into high tech when the nonalbum track "Head First," a Tyler/Perry/ Jim Vallance–penned *Get a Grip* outtake, was made available free of charge to subscribers to the CompuServe computer information network, who could download the entire song, in broadcast quality, free of charge (the band waived its publishing royalties for the occasion).

"If our fans are out there driving down that information superhighway, then we want to be playing at the truck stop," said Tyler. "This is the future—so let's get it going."

Indeed, the future once again seemed like an issue that was relevant for Aerosmith.

But before the band could move on to its future as a Sony recording act, there was still a contractual commitment to Geffen that needed to be honored. Towards that end, in November 1994, Geffen released *Big Ones*, a greatest-hits collection that combined the band's ten Geffen-era hits with the newly recorded "Blind Man" and "Walk on Water," along with "Deuces Are Wild," which had appeared on the various-artists album *The Beavis and Butthead Experience*. The two new tunes, produced by versatile New York veteran Michael Beinhorn, were recorded in New York and on Italy's Isle of Capri during the *Get a Grip* tour. The best-of album was accompanied by its video counterpart, *Big Ones You Can Look At*, which included the band's twelve Geffen videos with some new footage.

"As much as I love this album, and as good as it is, I can hear, just in my own contribution to it and the album as a whole, that we can do better," Tom Hamilton said of *Get a Grip*. "I'll look at it and say, 'We've got so much farther to go.'"

"When we started, we were so desperate to do what we're doing now," Whitford emphasized. "We've stayed true to those ideals. We came in with Hendrix and Cream records under our arms, and today we're still hungry to create the feeling we got from that music."

24

SHUT UP AND DANCE

In August 1994, Aerosmith capped the triumphant *Get a Grip* tour with an appearance at the two-day Woodstock '94 25th-anniversary festival in Saugerties, in upstate New York, sharing the bill with a startlingly diverse array of acts from all over the musical spectrum, including Alice In Chains, the Allman Brothers Band, Arrested Development, Crosby, Stills and Nash, Bob Dylan, Peter Gabriel, Metallica, the Red Hot Chili Peppers, Santana, and the Spin Doctors.

The Woodstock fest's uneasy mix of corporate sponsorship, cyberpunk culture and rock was underlined by a nasty backstage incident that transpired between Tim Collins and the event's co-producer, veteran New York-area promoter John Scher. Collins, already miffed that bill-mates Metallica were allowed to sell their own merchandise and use on-stage pyrotechnics (which Aerosmith had been forbidden to do), angrily confronted Scher after Scher refused to grant Collins an all-access pass. The argument apparently culminated with Scher throwing a bottle of Evian water across the room at Collins.

Aerosmith's inclusion on the bill seemed particularly appropriate. In the early seventies, the band's loud 'n' rude clamor had personified the lost generation of teenagers who'd come along in the wake of the hippie era. In the years since, Aerosmith survived the misadventures of its reckless youth to achieve a hard-won, late-blooming adulthood with unexpected dignity and respect. As such, the band in many ways personified rock 'n' roll's sometimes painful evolution from teenage distraction to lifelong commitment.

Writing in *Creem* in 1978, Robert Duncan pinpointed Aerosmith's fundamental appeal as "a feeling belonging to adolescence rather than childhood, in that there's some awareness of consequences, and is all the more exciting for it. It's a feeling to look for in rock 'n' roll."

For much of their career, Aerosmith produced music rooted in the presumption of extended adolescence and conducted their lives in the same way, ignoring the consequences of their choices for as long as they could get away with it. Once those consequences threatened to destroy their careers and their lives, the band finally opted for adulthood, but only after they'd exhausted all of their other options.

As the band prepares to begin the next phase of its career with the commencement of its Sony deal, Aerosmith's future, perversely enough, looks brighter than ever. "It's funny," says Steven Tyler. "I look at Tom and I go, 'Do we want to beat the shit out of ourselves and go on tour for another year?' Yes. What can I say?—we still love doing it the old-fashioned way."

"Make sure your love of what you're doing is really intense," Tom Hamilton advises those who would follow in Aerosmith's footsteps, "because if you love your music enough, it will get you through hopeless times and string the good ones together."

"It's not only about music," points out Joe Perry. "Being in a band is also about give and take, politics, educating yourself—music is your passion, but you cannot sustain a band on just that."

Commenting in the notes that accompanied *Pandora's Box,* Tyler noted, "The thing that really stands out in my mind about Aerosmith is that we're still fucking together. Whatever we've done together and whatever we've become, is second to the fact that we're still doing this. I'm still in love with these guys. I'm not saying it didn't take a lot of work, because drugs will take you and pull you apart. But it wasn't anything we shot up or put up our noses that gave us the edge—it was Joe Perry's fuck-all, being as abrasive as that motherfucker is, and Brad Whitford's ear, Tom Hamilton's well-aimed simplicity, and Joey Kramer's solid bed of backbeat. . . . So for all the music and all the other stuff that comes from Aerosmith, the most amazing thing is that we're still playing and still having some fucking fun.

"Is it love? Money? Hit records?" Tyler asked rhetorically. "You don't miss your water until the well runs dry and when we were at the bottom, I realized it wasn't any of that. It was about getting off on the band. That's all it's ever been."

"It's pretty weird for me to go to a radio station," observes Joe Perry. "You know how they'll have the CHR section and the AOR section and the oldies section? They'll all be playing us! It's scary sometimes. What will I be doing by the time I'm fifty? I don't know. All I can say is tomorrow I'm going to rock as hard as I did today. After that, who the fuck knows? I still have to get up, put on my pants and write a great song.

"We live it, breathe it, and bring it home," the guitarist concludes. "I can't believe I still love this shit."

"I don't buy into this idea that you're not supposed to rock 'n' roll after a certain date," Tyler said in a November 1994 *Rolling Stone* interview. "I'm looking to be the lounge act on the space shuttle so I can sing 'Walk This Way' on the ceiling."

Fans hoist the flag at Donington. (*Liane Hentscher/S.I.N.*)

25

WHAT IT TAKES

AEROSMITH ALBUMS (dates refer to original U.S. release)

Aerosmith, Columbia, January 1973.
Produced by Adrian Barber.
Make It; Somebody; Dream On; One Way Street; Mama Kin;
Write Me a Letter; Movin' Out; Walkin' the Dog.

Get Your Wings, Columbia, March 1974.
Produced by Jack Douglas and Ray Colcord.
Same Old Song and Dance; Lord of the Thighs; Spaced;
Woman of the World; S.O.S. (Too Bad); Train Kept A Rollin';
Seasons of Wither; Pandora's Box.

Toys in the Attic, Columbia, April 1975.

Produced by Jack Douglas.

Toys in the Attic; Uncle Salty; Adam's Apple; Walk This Way; Big Ten Inch Record; Sweet Emotion; No More No More; Round and Round; You See Me Crying.

Rocks, Columbia, May 1976.
Produced by Jack Douglas and Aerosmith.
Back in the Saddle; Last Child; Rats in the Cellar; Combination; Sick as a Dog; Nobody's Fault; Get the Lead Out; Lick and a Promise; Home Tonight.

Draw the Line, Columbia, December 1977.
Produced by Jack Douglas and Aerosmith.
Draw the Line; I Wanna Know Why; Critical Mass; Get It Up; Bright Light Fright; Kings and Queens; The Hand That Feeds; Sight for Sore Eyes; Milk Cow Blues.

Live Bootleg, Columbia, October 1978.
Produced by Jack Douglas and Aerosmith.
Back in the Saddle; Sweet Emotion; Lord of the Thighs; Toys in the Attic; Last Child; Come Together; Walk This Way; Sick as a Dog; Dream On; Chip Away the Stone; Sight for Sore Eyes; Mama Kin; S.O.S. (Too Bad); I Ain't Got You; Mother Popcorn; Train Kept A Rollin'/Strangers in the Night.

Night in the Ruts, Columbia, November 1979.
Produced by Gary Lyons and Aerosmith.
No Surprize; Chiquita; Remember (Walking in the Sand); Cheese Cake; Three Mile Smile; Reefer Head Woman; Bone to Bone (Coney Island Whitefish Boy); Think About It; Mia.

Aerosmith's Greatest Hits, Columbia, October 1980.
Various producers.
Dream On; Same Old Song and Dance; Sweet Emotion; Walk
This Way; Last Child; Back in the Saddle; Draw the Line; Kings
and Queens; Come Together; Remember (Walking in the
Sand).

Rock in a Hard Place, Columbia, August 1982.
Produced by Jack Douglas, Steven Tyler, and Tony Bongiovi.
Jailbait; Lightning Strikes; Bitch's Brew; Bolivian Ragamuffin;
Cry Me a River; Prelude to Joanie; Joanie's Butterfly; Rock in a
Hard Place (Cheshire Cat); Jig Is Up; Push Comes to Shove.

Done with Mirrors, Geffen, December 1985.
Produced by Ted Templeman.
Let the Music Do the Talking; My Fist Your Face; Shame On
You; The Reason a Dog; Shela; Gypsy Boots; She's On Fire;
The Hop; Darkness.

Classics Live!, Columbia, April 1986.
Produced by Paul O'Neill.
Train Kept A Rollin'; Kings and Queens; Sweet Emotion;
Dream On; Mama Kin; Three Mile Smile; Reefer Head Woman;
Lord of the Thighs; Major Barbara.

Classics Live! II, Columbia, June 1987.
Produced by Paul O'Neill and Aerosmith.
Back in the Saddle; Walk This Way; Movin' Out; Draw the
Line; Same Old Song and Dance; Last Child; Let the Music Do
the Talking; Toys in the Attic.

Permanent Vacation, Geffen, August 1987.

Produced by Bruce Fairbairn.

Heart's Done Time; Magic Touch; Rag Doll; Simoriah; Dude (Looks Like a Lady); St. John; Hangman Jury; Girl Keeps Coming Apart; Angel; Permanent Vacation; I'm Down; The Movie.

Gems, Columbia, November 1988.

Various producers.

Rats in the Cellar; Lick and a Promise; Chip Away the Stone; No Surprize; Mama Kin; Adam's Apple; Nobody's Fault; Round and Round; Critical Mass; Lord of the Thighs; Jailbait; Train Kept A Rollin'.

Pump, Geffen, September 1989.

Produced by Bruce Fairbairn.

Young Lust; F.I.N.E.; Going Down; Love in an Elevator; Monkey on My Back; Janie's Got a Gun; The Other Side; My Girl; Don't Get Mad, Get Even; Voodoo Medicine Man; What It Takes.

Pandora's Box, Columbia, November 1991.

Various producers.

When I Needed You [by Chain Reaction]; Make It; Movin' Out; One Way Street; On the Road Again; Mama Kin; Same Old Song and Dance; Train Kept A Rollin'; Seasons of Wither; Write Me a Letter; Dream On; Pandora's Box; Rattlesnake Shake; Walkin' the Dog; Lord of the Thighs; Toys in the Attic; Round and Round; Krawhitham; You See Me Crying; Sweet Emotion; No More No More; Walk This Way; I Wanna Know Why; Big Ten Inch Record; Rats in the Cellar; Last Child; All Your Love; Soul Saver; Nobody's Fault; Lick and a Promise;

Adam's Apple; Draw the Line; Critical Mass; Kings and Queens; Milk Cow Blues; I Live in Connecticut; Three Mile Smile; Let It Slide; Cheese Cake; Bone to Bone (Coney Island Whitefish Boy); No Surprize; Come Together; Downtown Charlie; Sharpshooter [by Whitford/St. Holmes]; Shit House Shuffle; South Station Blues [by the Joe Perry Project]; Riff & Roll; Jailbait; Major Barbara; Chip Away the Stone; Helter Skelter; Back in the Saddle.

Get a Grip, Geffen, April 1993.
Produced by Bruce Fairbairn.
Eat the Rich; Get a Grip; Fever; Livin' on the Edge; Flesh; Walk On Down; Shut Up and Dance; Cryin'; Gotta Love It; Crazy; Line Up; Amazing.

Big Ones, Geffen, November 1994.
Various producers.
Walk on Water; Love In An Elevator; Rag Doll; What It Takes; Dude (Looks Like a Lady); Janie's Got A Gun; Cryin'; Amazing; Blind Man; Deuces Are Wild; The Other Side; Crazy; Eat the Rich; Angel; Livin' on the Edge.

Box of Fire, Columbia, November 1994.
Various producers.
Includes the albums *Aerosmith, Get Your Wings, Toys in the Attic, Rocks, Draw the Line, Live Bootleg, Night in the Ruts, Aerosmith's Greatest Hits, Rock in a Hard Place, Classics Live!, Classics Live! II* and *Gems,* plus an additional disc containing the tracks Sweet Emotion 1991; Rockin' Pneumonia and the Boogie-Woogie Flu; Subway; Circle Jerk; Dream On (symphonic version).